CONCILIUM

Religion in the Eighties

CONCILIUM

Editorial Directors

Concilium 135 (5/1980): Fundamental Theology

TRUE AND FALSE UNIVERSALITY OF CHRISTIANITY

Edited by
Claude Geffré
and
Jean-Pierre Jossua

English Language Editor
Marcus Lefébure

T. & T. CLARK LTD.
Edinburgh

THE SEABURY PRESS
New York

May 1980
T. & T. Clark Ltd., 36 George Street, Edinburgh EH2 2LQ
ISBN: 0 567 30015 3

The Seabury Press, 815 Second Avenue, New York, N.Y. 10017
ISBN: 0 8164 2277 X

Library of Congress Catalog Card No.: 80 50479

Printed in Scotland by William Blackwood & Sons Ltd., Edinburgh

Concilium: Monthly except July and August.
Subscriptions 1980: All countries (except U.S.A. and Canada) £23·00 postage
and handling included; U.S.A. and Canada $54.00 postage and handling
included. (Second class postage licence pending at New York, N.Y.) Subscription
distribution in U.S. by Expediters of the Printed Word Ltd., 527 Madison
Avenue, Suite 1217, New York, N.Y. 10022.

CONTENTS

Part III
Some Major Implications

Part IV
Bulletins

Editorial

HOW TO affirm the universal vocation of the Church as a witness to the salvation of all men in Jesus Christ without falling into a false Christian universality which would encourage forms of intolerance and domination? This is the major question from which the present issue of *Concilium* starts.

The problem of the universality of Christianity is one of the most difficult questions Christian theology has to answer at a theoretical level. But today it has an urgent practical importance. Without mentioning the new positive assessment of the great non-Christian religions of the world since Vatican II, we can say that awareness of the historical particularity of Christianity has never been so alive. And we can add that a like awareness of a certain failure of its claim to universality has never been so plain and a discovery of the religious and cultural realities strange to the West has never been pushed so far.

How is it possible to claim that Christianity as a historical religion can lay hold of every man as the sole mediator of the relationship to the Absolute? This begins to seem excessive as soon as one discovers that the ways it has expressed itself doctrinally and ritually are obstacles to people born in a culture other than the Western one.

This is not a matter of doubting the universal scope of the Christ event as a historical manifestation of the eternal covenant between God and man. We must now, however, too rapidly use this claim about the universality of salvation in Jesus Christ as a pretext for refusing to look at the ambiguities involved in asserting that Christianity as a historical religion is universal in scope. We are today much more aware of the sometimes disastrous consequences in mission work of the theological axiom: 'Outside the Church, no salvation.' And our new consciousness of the relativity of Western civilisation should lead us to look squarely at the way in which the Church has tended to absolutise Western forms of Christianity. We have now a sufficient historical distance to be able better to discern a false universality tied to an apocalyptic conception of Christianity and to the expansive power of the West and the true universality of the Church which finds its sole legitimation in the particular figure of Jesus Christ as the universal mediator of salvation.

And it is probably a sign of the times that several articles in this issue testify to the search for a new Christian universalism tied to the liberation of the poor.

For lack of space, we have to limit ourselves here to presenting the articles in this issue succinctly and to trying to indicate the way they are linked together.

We thought it right to begin with a historical diagnosis of the gap between Christianity's claim to universality and factual reality. The author of the first article engages in a basic reflection on the discovery of 'ethnocentricity' and on the consequences of this for theology (W. Dupré). A second article faces us with some examples of absolute claims in the history of Christian missions. We see in particular that when proselytism goes hand in hand with a dominant political power it can lead to extreme forms of intolerance and of the conquest of souls by force (R. G. Cote). The next article describes the way in which the Church is facing the challenges of intellectual and spiritual pluralism in its defence of a universal natural law. What is interesting to note here is that a Church that avoids entering into specific details in the social field does not hesitate to frame very precise norms in the sexual field in the name of natural law.

The articles in the second part aim to contribute to a fundamental approach to the true universality of Christianity. It seemed right to begin by investigating the New Testament. Now it is quite clear that Jesus announced the good news in the first place to Israel, just as it is also certain that the first Christian preaching was very confined geographically, culturally and pastorally. The Church of the New Testament never, however, gave up proclaiming the God who wished the salvation of all men (J. Eckert). And since the notion of 'absolute religion' has often been invoked in order to justify the claim to the absolute on the part of the Christian mission, it seemed useful to present Hegel's authentic thinking on Christianity as an 'absolute religion'. Then, in a piece of fundamental theology, C. Duquoc seeks to disentangle the ways in which historic Christianity legitimated its claim to universality. He underlines the abuses to which the ecclesialogical axiom 'Outside the Church, no salvation' may have led and he seeks to bring out the original character of Christian universality founded on the particular figure of Jesus. It was left to a theologian from Latin America, J. Comblin, to testify that the debate about the true universality of Christianity is not an academic debate. Christians in Latin America know the cost of abandoning an abstract and traditional universalism and of discovering a new Christian universalism, the universalism of the freeing of the poor.

We then asked another author to show concretely why a universalist theology cast in the totalitarian mould has become out of the question today, and not only at the ecclesial level but at that of Christian existence. And on the basis of his pastoral experience in Africa, Monsignor Sanon sees in the local Church the place where the meeting between Christian universalism and cultural particularities can occur to the maximum advantage.

And finally, in the category of Bulletins, we have restricted ourselves to two testimonies: one on Jerusalem as a unique image of true Christian universality, that is to say, eschatological universality; the other about the absolute of the Gospel as that can be lived in the midst of other religious traditions such as Hinduism, Buddhism and Jainism (I. Puthiadam).

We are fully aware that this issue does no more than open up the way to a very tangled historical and theoretical terrain. But we should already have accomplished a lot if we succeeded in realising better that the historic Church can bear full witness to its universal vocation even though it gives up those claims to absolutism to which it tends to yield every time it forgets the distance there is between it and the kingdom to come.

Translated by John Maxwell

CLAUDE GEFFRÉ
JEAN-PIERRE JOSSUA

PART I

Towards a Historical Analysis

Wilhelm Dupré

Ethnocentrism and the Challenge of Cultural Relativity

IT IS a general experience that human beings tend to take their culture and its ideals as the standard that determines themselves and others. Though they might be ready to concede their own faults, they are nevertheless inclined 'to see one's in-group as always right and all out-groups as wrong whenever they differ' (Kroeber 1948: 266). It seems that the values and ideas by which we judge ourselves and the world around us are, in the first instance, idiosyncratic and culture bound, i.e., dependent on and equivalent to the mode of integration by which we discover ourselves as specific members of a community which, in turn, is part of a people whose language it speaks and whose way of life it adopts. Accordingly, if we may give a name to this attitude of measuring everything by the standards of one's own people or ethnos, it makes sense to follow the suggestion of W. G. Sumner and to speak of ethnocentrism (Sumner 1959 (1906): 13). Moreover, if we speak of ethnocentrism and yet are thinking of it as an attitude common among all human beings, it is obvious that we cannot do so without referring to cultural relativity, i.e., without pointing to a multitude of cultural forms in which ethnocentrism came to express and to oppose itself.

The fact that we are capable of making such an observation is, of course, a most remarkable and noticeable experience which should not be left out when we discuss ethnocentrism. As such it indicates what ethnocentrism is about in the second instance. I shall resume this problem later on. What I would like to emphasise at this point is the factual confirmation of ethnocentric perception and evaluation as primary categories of man's encounter with himself and with reality, and of cultural relativity as the necessary outcome of this encounter (see F. L. K. Hsu 1979: 517 ff).

3

In the following I will try to outline the significance of these categories for the evaluation of cultures as well as for the status of theoretical thinking with respect to personal and cultural reality. To accomplish this goal I will start with the emergence and the discovery of ethnocentrism. By checking the background of ethnocentrism and its discovery I will then ask for the parameters that answer to the conceptual demands of universality and of man's search for truth. Finally, I will discuss some of the consequences that follow from the awareness of cultural relativity and the idea of universality. It is my conviction that any attempt to find and to realise the truth and dignity of man is bound to accept and to acknowledge cultural relativity, and to reject any position that refuses to discuss its own ethnocentric dimensions.

1. THE DISCOVERY OF ETHNOCENTRISM

Ever since human beings have been in contact with different peoples they felt obliged to account for the fact of their existence. If we evaluate this attitude in the light of ethnocentrism, there is no reason to be surprised. For, by the same token by which it is taken for granted that—as it is the case among many peoples—the name of 'man' designates that of the particular people as well, it is obvious that the existence of beings which are at once similar and dissimilar must be seen as a challenge to one's own identity, especially when it is not only a question of economical and technological issues, but of ethical and religious truths.

Indeed, if we consult culture history, we can easily see that there are basically two or, if we take their combination as a separate one, three solutions to this problem. Either one works with a temporal model wherein the same events in the beginning account for one's own position as well as for that of other peoples, or one adopts a spatial model, wherein the distance to one's own central position is equivalent to the cultural differences and their significance, or one employs a combination of both models.

To give examples: in the first instance one could think, of peoples who explain their own situation by stories, in which 'early' family tensions or other events resulted in the differentiation of and the differences among the descendants. In the second instance, one could think of traditions for which the distinction between their own people and the 'barbarians' or between the civilised and the uncivilised world functions as a basis for the evaluation of others. And finally, one could think of those situations where the label of the 'barbarian' and that of the 'heathen', i.e., of a being whose position is ultimately determined by sacred history, are interchangeably used to evaluate ethical and religious differences.

There can be no doubt that the ethnocentric perspective as it comes forth in this context displays all the qualities that are proper to myth. As a matter of fact, if we approach it from the opposite direction, i.e., if we pay attention to the historical circumstances under which one becomes aware of such a perspective at all, it is either the quest for religious and cultural universality or the concern with the idea of justice which exposes the claims of ethnocentrism. That means that we are referred to situations where mythologies have become questionable and (or) where the demands of the logos are held against those of mythos.

If we take for instance the famous statement of Xenophanes: 'If oxen or lions had hands which enabled them to draw and paint pictures as men do, they would portray their gods as having bodies like their own; horses would portray them as horses and oxen as oxen' (Wheelright 1966: 33), it is obvious that his own tradition had ceased to provide the overall perspective that it used to give. On the other hand, by searching for an acceptable explanation, he comes to the conclusion that people do not describe reality as it is, though that is what they claim to do, but as they see it, depending on the particular circumstances of their nature and tradition.

Or we may think of Nicolaus Cusanus who, because of his insight into the relativity of the observer and the logic of learned ignorance (Cusanus 1964: 394 ff) came to the conclusion that habit is no substitute for truth and that religious convictions had to be judged in the light of their presuppositions rather than on the basis of their face values (Cusanus 1967: 718 ff).

And finally with respect to our own age, it should be noted that the discussion about ethnocentrism and the formulation of ethical and cultural relativism as a response to this problem remain unintelligible if we do not see them in conjunction with the cultural or mythological consciousness of Western man. Of course, there remains the fact that the exposition of ethnocentrism and the promotion of ethical and cultural relativism cannot be thought without a deepened knowledge of other cultures and the subjection to the rules of knowledge. But if we study for instance, E. Westermarck (1906) as one of the main exponents of ethical relativism, or M. Herskovits (1973) as the most influential representative of cultural relativism, we become easily aware that the study of fact is also correlated with issues of a new world orientation as well as of social, political and international justice (see T. Lemaire 1976, R. Ginters 1978).

In other words, to the extent that practical motives assume the form of theoretical symbols and that theoretical considerations rely on the enactment of cultural goals, the conclusion is warranted that the discussion of ethnocentrism is not only a matter of scientific interest but of cultural self-identification as well. As such it assumes functions which traditionally have been reserved for mythology. Even more important, it evokes a tradition similar to the one that originally gave birth to philosophy as an attempt to realise the truth of existence by connecting it with the existence of truth as the reality of thought and freedom alike.

2. THE TWO PARAMETERS OF ETHNOCENTRISM

The association of ethnocentrism with myth and cultural self-identification on the one hand, and with the awareness of this juncture on the other hand, is significant in at least two ways. In the first place it gives us an idea about the dialectical character of this problem. In the second place, it gives us an indication that the solution to the problem might be found within the problem itself.

If it is true for instance, that our thinking unfolds relative to the culture wherein it becomes articulate, then it is also true that the conception of ethnocentrism is culture specific, i.e., ethnocentric. The same holds true when we consider cultural relativism. As a perspective that evolved in a particular cultural constellation it is as much culture dependent as any other judgment about man and reality. It is, as Cook has shown, an ethnocentric notion (1978: 289).

Similarly, if we consider ethical relativism as a theory that applies its conclusions to itself it either turns against its own intuition by becoming an ethnocentric judgement about other cultures, or it loses its subject-matter because it does not know what it is talking about.

Or more generally: if the logos by which we discern and oppose the mythologies of ethnocentrism recognises the conditions under which it becomes operative, it cannot reject its own ethnocentric origin. On the contrary, if the logos of ethnocentrism disregards its dependence on ethnocentric mythologies, it is bound to become a myth by itself. When seen from the viewpoint of univocal distinctions, there is no way to escape the trappings of ethnocentrism

Since the meaning of the one position refers us to the opposite in order to be maintained, there can be no mistake about the dialectical character of this problem. Yet, what does it mean that we are able to make statements like these? What does it mean that we are capable of perceiving other cultures and of adjusting our thinking to this perception?

I have mentioned already that the realisation of this problem is an experience that speaks for itself by providing its own factuality (see Dupré 1973: 12 ff). As such it offers us a vantage point where the opposition between subjectivity and objectivity, between cultural dependence and independence becomes irrelevant, because the factuality of this experience vindicates itself whenever we affirm or deny it, argue for or against it. In other words, while we attend to the possible relationships between man and culture we discover in this attention the emergence of a mode of knowledge that holds its own grounds by being turned toward itself, or, if we want, by referring to its own being. As such it does not need any justification, because justification concurs with its constitution.

The appeal to this experience, however, remains an empty gesture as long as we take it only as an isolated instance that concerns nothing but knowledge itself. On the other hand, if we take it as an event that happens within culture history, the formal relationship with knowledge reveals itself as a mediatory one: we discover that it is a cultural being that knows and that it is cultural reality which comes forth as the result of this event. What presented itself as a vantage point turns out to be a focal point as well which enables us to extend the validity of the former to what is brought into focus by the latter.

There are two conclusions which we may draw from these deliberations. The first is that of the transcultural unity of the cultural universe itself. The second concerns the human person and its independence with respect to this universe.

Since movement and result of ethnocentric experiences are mediated in the experience of these experiences, the unity of the latter pertains to that of the former as well. To the extent, however, that this unity cannot be thought of without the essential difference of knowledge itself we have to retain this difference when talking about the cultural universe. As a result, we can state that any particular culture refers to the cultural universe but does not become identical with it. Paradoxical as it might sound, if we consider the cultural particularity of ethnocentrism in the light of the culture concept, it is the cultural universe itself which, as transcultural unity of all that is limited and idiosyncratic, comes into focus.

In contrast to the unity of the cultural universe which begins to appear when cultural reality is seen in conjunction with the concept of culture, the unity of the human person has to be established before the existence of many cultures becomes an issue. As we all know, there will be no articulation if there is nobody who articulates. By recalling the energy of articulation rather than its results, it becomes obvious that the movement toward the unity of the cultural universe reverses itself by focusing on man as the representative of this universe. What we observe is, so to speak, an inflection of the cultural universe which, by being mediated in particular situations, emerges in the human person both as part of and as a reality apart from definite cultures. Moreover, since the thrust of this movement corresponds, though in terms of inversion, with that of the cultural universe, it is man as a person who comes forth as another transcultural entity. As such he precedes culture ontologically no matter

B

how poor and limited he may be otherwise. Being a person, man is indeed the measure of all things. But while he measures everything, it should be kept in mind that it is his own being which is also setting him apart from his creations. From the viewpoint of the human person it is not the concept which anticipates the unity of particular realities, but the reality of particular unities which recalls the conceptual or universal character of their beginning. Accordingly, if we address man as the measure of everything, we actually have to point to the cultural universe as the standard of his creations and to himself as their meaning and fulfilment.

So far we have tried to make use of the vantage point that came into being when we reflected upon the experience of ethnocentric experiences. By referring to the transcultural unity of the cultural universe and by relying upon the human person as an equally transcultural entity that anticipates cultural reality in its own being, we can now state that we have found two parameters which enable us to understand the constitution of ethnocentric perspectives and to judge their validity and truth both from within such a perspective and with respect to their cross-cultural significance.

They enable us to understand ethnocentrism because neither of them can be thought of without the connecting meaning of universality as the actual force of all that falls between them. What ever we do as human beings recalls the universal significance of the human person and anticipates the unity of a reality which comprises everything that is cultural. Our deeds assume the form of validity. They are either good or bad, meaningful or senseless. They are examples meant to be repeated and, therefore, subject to the judgment of possible repetition. Man is forced to appear as an ethnocentric being but free to recognise the limitations of this appearance.

They enable us to judge about ethnocentrism because, on the one hand, they relativise its claims whenever we forget that they are not identical with the cultural universe or fall short of the dignity of the person. On the other hand, by focusing themselves upon the ethnocentric expressions of universality, they provide an internal standard for an evaluation of cultures with respect to themselves as well as to one another.

Moreover, while the relationship of necessity and freedom as it becomes visible within this context underlines once more the dialectical character of ethnocentric positions, it is the affirmation and the concept of necessity as well as of freedom which permit us to break through the trappings of ethnocentrism and to search for the truth of being under the conditions of human existence. To reach this goal we do not have to leave the ethnocentric perspective of our own tradition as long as we accept the double parameter of the cultural universe and the human person. In face of other cultures, however, it would by myopic and contrary to the search for truth, if we did not subject our own ethnocentric perspective to the judgment of these cultures. In this respect we must not restrict our conscience to what we see, but have to extend our consciousness to what is visible at all in order to comply with the demands of truth and universality. Whether we accept the perspective of innocent ethnocentrism or let ourselves be forced into its dialectical development, whether we adopt an absolute but blind ethnocentrism, relativise it within the constellation of necessity and freedom, is not a question of academic curiosity, but of truth and its concrete manifestations in human beings and cultural realities. It is a response to the challenge of relativity both as an opposition to and as an expression of truth.

3. ETHNOCENTRISM AND THE MEANING OF THEOLOGY

While the factual coexistence of cultures and peoples gave rise to ethnocentric perspectives that accounted for their existence in terms of myth and mythological evidence, the discovery of ethnocentrism has partially been the outcome of the logos as it opposed the evidences of mythos and mythological traditions, and partially of experiences in which one encountered cultures whose existence had not been known so far and whose reality did not unequivocally answer to the established patterns of expectation. At the same time it has to be noted, however, that the discovery of ethnocentrism did not result in its abolition. On the contrary, new forms of ethnocentrism became the order of the day.

If we ask for the reasons of ethnocentrism, there can be no doubt that it is the consciousness of and the quest for universality which lie at the root of the problem. Since man is a speaking being, the world around him does not stay the way it is, but is actually transformed into the synthesis of symbols and a symbolic milieu. As such it shares in the universality of meaning, but expresses it in the particularities of specific situations. Since the universality of the human presence comes forth in the particularity of specific words, deeds, values, and so forth, the perception of the world is bound to take place within an ethnocentric perspective. As a result, there is no way to avoid ethnocentrism.

To the extent, however, that the idea of universality applies to the process in which it becomes operative, the ethnocentric perspective in itself is no closed issue, but a question of adequacy and truth. Moreover, since the implication and the reference of the ethnocentric perspective, i.e., the human person and the cultural universe, are not exhausted by their syntheses, they not only enable us to evaluate this perspective while being part of it, but also permit us to identify other perspectives and to compare them with our own in such a way that we accept them on their own grounds and as a challenge to the truth that we believe to have found (see W. Dupré 1975: 331 ff).

If we evaluate theology in the light of these deliberations, we see at once that they are highly relevant both for the cultural indentification of this discipline and with respect to its function as the conscience of the religious community. No matter how we define theology, if we insist on its universality, it is only logical when we confront it with its own cultural situation and whatever follows on a cross-cultural level. If we insist on its uniqueness, we cannot close our eyes to the fact that there are other theologies that do the same. In any case, the conviction that we know how other cultures should be evaluated does not free us from the task of asking for the ethnocentric qualities of this knowledge.

But as much as there should not be any doubt about the ethnocentric character of theology, we should know that the answer to this problem cannot be sought in a theological relativism that joins the proclaimed theories of ethical and cultural relativism. Since these theories are blind to their own myth, they do not, as has been pointed out already, overcome the ethnocentric shortcomings, but add only to their modification. The same holds true if we absolutise a particular theology. No matter whether it concerns culture, ethics, or theology, if all we accept is our own system, we cannot avoid turning it into one of many systems. What claims to be absolute without a recollection of its relativity falls, though under a different name, under the category of ethnocentric myopia.

In contrast to the proclaimed theories of relativism there is, however, the discovery of relativity as an equivalent to that of ethnocentrism. What counts in this discovery is not the apparent or real contradiction of statements, but the fact that the truth of man is above all a question of the concretion of personal and cultural existence. In other words, when we evaluate the meaning of ethnocentrism we should draw a clear line between the observation of cultural relativity and the conclusions we develop on the basis of this observation. Within this context the concept of relativity is not a substitute for, but a critical assessment of universalism. If it is meant to be a substitute, the result is hypocrisy on the theoretical level and disdain on the practical level.

What then, is the lesson that theology is taught by the discovery of ethnocentrism?

In the first instance I would like to express a warning against any kind of parochial thinking. The point is that there are not only noticeable differences between various cultures and religions which, if for no other reason than that of their existence, should be taken into consideration, but that the same evaluative patterns return in different situations. The awareness of this fact is reason enough to exempt nothing from reconsideration. If we are afraid to do so, the fear of error becomes in fact, and as Hegel has pointed out (Hegel 1952: 65) fear of truth, while the belief in ultimate truth perverts into the assumption that nothing but the 'system' can save us.

In the second place I would like to point to the meaning of tolerance. If we comprehend culture in the light of ethnocentrism and the conditions of its existence, we have to expect that the manifestation of truth is definitely not that of uniformity in the sense of indefinitely repeated particularities. On the contrary, as long as the human person is more than a construction, and the cultural universe more than the cultures it is composed of, there has to be variety, both with respect to the perspectives that make us see and to the judgments we form within the framework of such perspectives. Yet, while we affirm cultural relativity in the name of truth, we should not forget the reason for this affirmation as expressed by the idea of tolerance. In this respect we can also say that it is the practical quality of personal existence, or, if we see it in the light of universality, of personal uniqueness and dignity, and, to the extent that a particular culture is subject to the unity of the cultural universe, of cultural harmony, which become critical for the meaning of tolerance and its theoretical transformation.

In the third place I would like to stress the need for theology to integrate the culture concept into its theory formation. Though it is the purpose of theoretical thinking to subject itself and its objects to the idea of universality, the task itself has to be realised by means of cultural entities, i.e., of symbols. As a result, it is not only by dint of universality, but also because of the means by which the goal is to be obtained that theoretical efforts turn out to be cultural phenomena. Conversely, if the purpose of theoretical thinking is to be realised, we cannot dismiss cultural relativity in order to conceptualise the truth of man and the world wherein he lives and dies—a world which is at least partially the outcome of his own doings. Just as a church that negates the essential presence of culture-specific elements in the constitution of its being is bound to become idolatrous because of the implicit deification of its finite existence, theology is bound to miss its truth, if it refuses the insights that the discovery of ethnocentrism has forced upon us.

In the fourth place I would like to emphasise the ontological priority of the person and his tradition. To do so is not only important with respect to the legitimation of churches, but also for the acceptance of faith as a principle of theory. It is important for the churches because it justifies the recollection of this reality in terms of institutional organisation. And for theory, because it connects it with the reality of truth as it has come to exist in personal relations and attitudes. The recollection of personal reality and its consequences is, however, only one side of the medal. The other side concerns its significance as a criterion of truth. For, while the task of theology might be described as the attempt to situate the mystery of God and man in culture history and to draw out its meaning in terms of ultimate validity, it is the concrete universality of personal and cultural existence which judges the judgments of theory and praxis alike. In other words, while theology is compelled by its theoretical energy to articulate a judgment about man and culture, it is the cultural existence of personal beings which decides about the adequacy of this judgment. Since this existence has found its expressions in a variety of cultural constellations, the study of these constellations is not only a question of theoretical orientation but also of the internal verification procedure without which theology too, is doomed to remain meaningless.

Finally I would like to point to the idea and the articulation of local theologies and liturgies both as response to the challenge of cultural relativity and as a criterion for breaking through the self-sufficiency of ethnocentrism, especially when it concerns a religion that understands its own centricity as a world-wide mission. As such they are not a matter of synchretistic combinations but the expression of truth as it exists and is to be pursued under the conditions of culture history. Within the Church they testify to the Church's correspondence with the principles of its own being, i.e., to a Church which does not identify itself in terms of domination, but of communion in accordance with the demands of personal dignity, freedom, and holiness.

If we assess the eschatological chances of our age, we cannot dismiss the legitimate claims of personal existence and cultural reality. Though until now the discovery of ethnocentrism has resulted in an interpretation of cultural relativism that seemed to be the death knell of universality, we have come to understand today that matters are more complicated than that. While we face the dilemma of losing the meaning of otherness because we absolutise ethnocentrism, and of sameness, because we absolutise relativity, we cannot avoid the insight that universality is neither a matter of absolutisatism, nor a matter of relativisation, but of both. As such it forces us to radicalise our thinking once more in order to affirm man's fundamental relationship with universality and truth, and to search for its meaning in terms that concur with the possibilities of our own age. Within this context, theology stands to win or to lose its credibility, depending on whether it rejects or accepts the challenge of cultural relativity.

Bibliography:

Cook, J., 'Cultural relativism as an ethnocentric notion' in R. Beehler, A. Drengson *The Philosophy of Society* (London 1978).

Cusanus, N., *De docta ignorantia. Schriften I* (Vienna 1964); *De pace fidei. Shriften III* (Vienna 1967).

Dupré W., 'The Hermeneutical Significance of Culture' in *Proceedings of the American Catholic Philosophical Association:* 48 (1973) 12-20; *Religion in Primitive Cultures: A Study in Ethnophilosophy* (The Hague 1975).

Ginters, R., *Relativismus in der Ethik* (Düsseldorf 1978).

Hegel, G. W. F., *Phänomenologie des Geistes* (Hamburg 1952).

Herskovits, M., *Cultural Relativism: Perspectives in Cultural Pluralism* (ed. F. Herskovits) (New York 1973).

Hsu, F. L. K., 'The Culture Problem of the Cultural Anthropologist' in *American Anthropologist:* 81 No 3 (1979) 517-532.

Kroeber, A. L., *Anthropology* (New York 1948).

Lemaire, T., *Over de waarde van kulturen* (Baarn 1976).

Sumner, W. G., *Folkways* (New York 1959 [1906]).

Westermarck, E., *The Origin and Development of the Moral Ideas* (London 1906).

Wheelright, Ph., *The Presocratics* (New York 1966).

Richard Cote

Some Pretensions to the Absolute in the History of Christian Missions

IN THEORY, Christianity absolutises neither the finite, the conditional, nor the relative in anything human—even in religion. In practice, however, it has often pursued its mission in the course of history as though the opposite were true. To diagnose the presuppositions behind some of the past missionary pretensions to the absolute is not an easy task. First, because such an exercise invariably leads back to the need for reflection on those fundamental questions which Church historians have only asked infrequently, and then mostly in passing. These concern what really goes on in the lives of missionaries, the actual (often hidden) motives, goals, prejudices and events that determine their missionary choices and commitments. The fact of missionary expansion is plain enough, but the underlying issue of what motivated it at a given point in time is far from clear. Indeed to analyse missionary motivation can be a task as delicate as analysing the chemical composition of a perfume, with its multiple ingredients—some of which are invariably latent, while others, sniffed in isolation, would make us wince.

A second difficulty of course concerns our ability to read and interpret the past 'authentically'. Our modern historical consciousness makes us very much aware of the fact that even the most 'authentic' interpretation of the past must be considerably relativised, and this includes, ironically, our reading of the Church's historical pretensions to the absolute. As Michel de Certeau observed some years ago, *'En changeant, nous changeons le passé'*. Despite these limitations, however, it is still possible to identify certain areas of the missionary enterprise in which the Church

14

did lend itself very readily to the admission and interplay of some misguided pretensions to the absolute. Our attention will focus on the
question of proselytism and that of missionary adaptation.

1. MISSIONARIES AND PROSELYTISM

One of the most persistent of missionary habits from early Christianity
to the latter part of the nineteenth century, is the division that was drawn
between Christians and pagans. This regrettable dichotomy split the
world into two unequal, fundamentally opposite spheres and brought
forth more myths, more detailed ignorance and more ambitions than any
other perception of difference. Christians were sure that only baptised
and orthodox believers would attain God: others would go to hell. Underlying this pessimistic outlook was the conviction that 'Outside the Church
there is no salvation', a formula that was first interpreted in an absolute,
exclusive sense. Even in its more lenient form, this ecclesiology maintained that outside the Church salvation was at best difficult and pre-
carious, and that those not in the Church lived in dangerous darkness and
separation from God. Hence one of the main motives of the missionary
impulse was to rescue as may of the heathen as possible from the everlasting damnation that otherwise awaited them. Implicit in this, of course,
was a deep compassion for one's fellow man that accounts for so many
heroic lives and deeds in the missionary enterprise. But the real power of
this 'necessary-for-salvation' motive rested upon keeping it absolute.
Once any mitigating interpretation is admitted of either 'necessary' or
'salvation', the force of the motive declines.

One need only think of St Francis Xavier, the patron of missions,
baptising thousands of people because he was convinced that if he did not
do so they would be doomed to hell. The same spirit motivated the
sixteenth-century Jesuits in Brazil; they conceived their task primarily in
terms of bringing light and salvation to peoples who were in error and
where souls were being lost. It is clear from their letters that even when
they brought the Indians together in separate villages, this was not so
much to create an indigenous Christian community but to save as many
individual souls as possible. Numerical growth was to become so central a
criterion that it alone served as an index for judging the success of a
mission. Indeed the Church has always had considerable difficulty in
resolving the question of the proper relationship between its relative
position *in* the world and its universal mission *to* the world. All too
frequently it identified its supposed mission to the whole world with
numerical gains. And in the realm of missionary activity, absolute universality dreamt of as an actual possibility is a dangerous idol: it can raise
up missionary zealots who forge for it instruments of the worst spiritual

imperialism. This tendency has existed in the history of Christian missions and it makes little difference if the missionaries are eighth-century Franks, sixteenth-century Spaniards, nineteenth-century British or twentieth-century Americans. Proselytism, when practised by those associated with a dominating political force, can justify colonial adventures and the use of force in propagating the faith among unwilling infidels. The point is obvious: where the universal claim of a religion is supported by and supports the civil power, the best possible groundwork is laid for intolerance—that unmistakable sign of pretensions to the absolute and the illusory dream of a wholly Catholic world. The object of the exercise itself thus comes to be described in military terms: 'winning' converts. One scores a victory; a new conquest bringing another medal to add to one's glory.

The most extreme example of this is the phenomenon of 'forced conversions', a phenomenon that recurs with embarrassing frequency in the history of Christian missions. In the sixth century Pope Gregory the Great urged Ethelbert of Kent and the nobility of Sardinia to use force, if necessary, to convert their pagan peasants. In the seventh century St Amand, the first real missionary to Flanders, obtained a royal order enforcing baptism on pagans. In the eighth century Charlemagne forced the Old Saxons and the prince of Moravia to be baptised. In the ninth century King Olaf of Norway forced the gospel on the majority of his subjects with every kind of violence. In the twelfth century the Swedes conquered and forced the Catholic faith on the Finns. And the abuses committed in this regard by the Crusaders are too well known to be dealt with here.

This legacy of intolerance and forced conversions was carried over into the 'age of discovery' with a more subtle but no less intimate connection between colonialism and proselytism. Early exploration was once again dominated by that curious intermixture of religion and material aims in which the infidels' losses became the believers' gains. The *Requerimiento,* for example, a manifesto devised by Martin de Enciso in 1513 and given full papal support, required the Indians to recognise the Church 'as sovereign and mistress of the whole world'. Should they refuse to submit to the Christian religion, their masters had the right to reduce them to slavery, dispossess them of their property, and treat them as badly as possible. Thus when America was first colonised, the opinion was widely held that because of their paganism the heathen had no spiritual and civil rights. Others, more charitable, declared that the enslavement of the negro was an act of mercy, because only through slavery could large numbers be brought to Christ. Typically, the French *Code Noir* of 1685 obliged every planter to have his negroes baptised and properly instructed in the Christian faith. Nor was this decree to remain a dead letter; among others Bienville enforced it shortly after he founded New Orleans in 1718.

In order to understand this kind of proselytism and the stout-hearted pretensions to the absolute which undergirded it, one must probe more deeply and ask why such developments were possible. First, there was the burning desire among many missionaries of the time to establish a New Jerusalem in America. Protestantism had shattered the unity of Christendom in Europe and as a result, many Spaniards yearned to accomplish in the New World a new spiritual conquest. Many writers then and later pointed out that Luther and Cortez had been born in the same year, one to destroy Christian unity in Europe and the other to make possible a new world free from the religious dissensions that were splitting the old world asunder. To achieve this dream the souls of the Indians had to be won on the basis of a massive approach, even if this necessitated the use of some force and coercion. Secondly, there was the close union between the mission and colonial imperialism, a union that was epitomised in the maxim *Cuius regio, eius et religio*. The Peace of Augsburg (1555) practically left it to the omnipotent prince to decide what religion his subjects should profess. Crown and Cross seemed natural allies and hence princes conceived it their duty to spread the faith. But as the history of Christian expansion demonstrates, the weapons proper to princes are not likely to be those proper to saints. Thirdly, another factor which gave rise to certain pretensions to the absolute and which made tolerance seem like betrayal was the fierce loyalties peculiar to the nationalism of the time. As Pope Pius XI was to say in 1929: 'Nationalism has always been a plague upon the missions. It is not too much to call it a malediction.'

Such extraneous motives were even more unfortunate because they allowed totally well-intentioned missionaries to engage enthusiastically in an activity, completely oblivious to the harm that they were doing and unable to evaluate realistically what they were in fact achieving. It is curious and doubtless revealing that the writings of most pioneer mission theorists of the sixteenth and seventeenth centuries (Acosta, Thomas a Jesu, Brancati and Gubernatis) reveal an ambiguous posture with regard to the use of force in winning souls. On the one hand, they could justify the Spanish imperial policies and ask rhetorically: 'How could these barbaric peoples possibly be restrained and tamed unless they feared the military might of the Spanish?' On the other hand, however, they were all equally convinced that the missionaries themselves should refrain from using force to propagate the faith. This ambiguous posture, with its inherent contradictions and fateful consequences, points up the fact that Christian missions have never been neutral or independent of the dominant ideology and milieu from which they have come. This is especially true when numerical gains or quantitative Church growth is regarded as 'the chief task' of mission. Yet there were others, like Las Casas, Victoria and Veracruz, who fought stoutly for the rights of the indigenous people and who condemned many of the historical extremes that resulted in the practice of proselytism.

2. MISSIONARY ADAPTATION

A second major area in which the absolutist claims of the Church have surfaced in the history of Christian missions is that of missionary adaptation—or more precisely, the lack of it. In recent times, many young Churches in the Third World have rejected the policy of missionary adaptation as being paternalistic and completely out-of-date; it is viewed as a 'tactical ploy' on the part of the older Churches, an 'obliging' or 'accommodating' overture that not only fails to do justice to the intrinsic meaning and value of local customs, but also one that betrays a phony universalism. In 1974, for example, the bishops of Africa and Madagascar rejected the theology of adaptation in favour of a more radical policy of incarnation, that is, one that does not merely pay lip-service to the principle of indigenisation. The challenge confronting these Churches is very clear: How is Western Christianity's traditional understanding and practice of the faith to be reconciled with an entirely new awareness of the intrinsic value and validity of the diverse human cultures through which Christianity is supposed to become incarnate, contemporary, relevant and Catholic? The traditional policy of missionary adaptation has been devalued as a result of the abuses done in its name. It has become more and more obviously true that the superficial half-measures of adaptation frequently precluded the possibility of genuine incarnation and therefore real authenticity. Indeed the very term itself presupposes that there is already in existence, fully constituted, a universal law which one then 'adapts' to varying local conditions and customs.

The policy of missionary adaptation need not imply a phony universalism, however, if it is seriously and unstintingly adopted in practice. Such was the case when the early Church entered thoroughly into the cultural life of the Roman empire. Without sacrificing the essentials of its doctrine the missionary Church preserved from the old culture whatever was good, transformed whatever was indifferent, and in the hope of a gradual process of purification even tolerated much that was considered evil, but not intrinsically or irremediably so. It was cultural accommodation carried to its highest point. To have attempted to impose upon Roman society Jewish cultural forms would have doomed the missionary enterprise from the start. Any hope of breathing a new Christian soul into the highly developed body of Roman society required a policy of the broadest possible accommodation on the part of the Church.

It is true that the Fathers of the Church spoke most disparagingly about the pagan religious customs of their day. They believed that all the gods of the gentiles were demons and that the souls of the pagans were enslaved by Satan. But this negative judgment was more rhetorical than real. Indeed, if not always in words, the Fathers were far more accommodating toward pagan values than their strident rhetoric would indicate. We see this, for example, in the way they retained their personal names, many of them originating in pagan mythology, the frequency with which they borrowed both terminology and symbols from pagan religions, and their eagerness to find in the philosophy and the sibylline oracles of the time a confirmation of Christian doctrine. Moreover the Fathers genuinely believed that the so-called 'pagan' heart was not corrupt but basically good, suitable material for Christianisation (*anima naturaliter Christiana*). During the following centuries, as the Germanic tribes became Christians, the practice of employing traditional rites and customs to express Christian beliefs was continued. As Professor Latourette has shown in his *History of the Expansion of Christianity,* the practice was strongly encouraged by both the missionaries and the Church leaders of the time, including such outstanding figures as Boniface, Cyril and Methodius, Gregory the Great, and Augustine. The Draconian Saxon policics of Charlemagne, the first to seriously distort the role of the temporal power in missionary work, was an exception to the enlightened methods of accommodation so characteristic of the time.

As the age of discoveries dawned, however, the policy of missionary adaptation was almost invariably abandoned and with its disappearance, a wave of false pretensions to the absolute emerged in the Church—a wave that would eventually come to a crest in the nineteenth century. Europe was regarded as the home of everything that was good, civilised, and Christian, while missionary work was looked upon as an all-out war on 'savagery' and 'superstition'. Church leaders and missionaries insisted upon a fairly total identification of Christianity and Western cultural forms and values. The approach generally adopted was a frontal attack on pagan customs. We see this in Africa, for example, when the Portuguese missionaries went to Benin in 1538 and the Spanish Capuchins to the Congo a century later. The same was true in Ethiopia. Immediately after the conversion of the Emperor Susenyos in 1622, the missionaries embarked on a full-scale onslaught on all the points of ritual, doctrine and practice which separated the Ethiopian Church and Rome. This cultural and theological arrogance provoked a national reaction: Susenyos was forced to abdicate and in 1632 his successor expelled the missionaries.

The same high-handed approach was used in India. Here the absolutist mentality of the Church was enhanced and even galvanised into law by the secular political power of the day. All Mohammedan and pagan priests, penitents and sorcerers were driven from areas under Portuguese domination; non-Christian places of worship were to be destroyed; public practice of any but the Christian religion was forbidden; polygamy was punishable by banishment to the galleys; and certain sections of the city were zoned against non-Christians. These laws and decrees, which were issued in the latter half of the sixteenth century, reveal a great deal about the dangerous type of Eurocentricism that prevailed at the time. Christian life was modelled in almost every detail upon that of Portugal. Converts were thoroughly Portugalised, obliged to take Portuguese names, wear Portuguese clothes, and observe Portuguese customs. Even the native clergy were educated entirely on the European model. Furthermore, they were treated as a kind of second class clergy, little more than catechists. Nor was there any appreciation of their unique qualifications as interpreters of Indian thought. In short, the Western forms of Christianity were imposed as absolute, and as universally normative.

Towards the end of the sixteenth century a small group of Jesuit missionaries in China broke with the dominant spirit of the times and tried to revive methods of cultural adaptation which had played so prominent a part in the earlier centuries of Christian expansion. With a great deal of empathy and tact, Matteo Ricci entered quietly into the body of Chinese culture and attempted to open channels along which the gospel could penetrate Chinese intellectual life. His methods, however, gave rise to the protracted Chinese rites controversy after his death which was finally decided against him by Clement XI in 1704 and 1715. On 11 July, 1742, Benedict XIV again forbade any toleration of the rites and banned further debate under pain of severe ecclesiastical penalties, a condemnation that was to remain in force for more than 200 years.

During this moratorium, the ingrained tendency to absolutise, almost eternalise many of the Western forms of Christianity, permeated the entire missionary enterprise. Even the minority of missionaries who understood both the meaning of culture and the importance of adaptation seldom looked beyond the superficial stage of drums and pagoda roofs; and most of them were not even allowed to go that far. By the nineteenth century, therefore, when the Church experienced one of its greatest periods of missionary expansion, the majority of missionaries had no doubt about the complete superiority of their own Western culture. Their method, by and large, was to transplant all they could of Christianity in its Western forms. Little or no thought was given to the provisional nature of the Church's 'garb', the mutability of its norms, and the adaptability of its rites. It was not until Pius XI, and then only in the last years of his pontificate, that the principle of missionary adaptation was revived, and promoted. Indeed the greatest number of historical and theological studies ever to be written on the subject appeared during these years and those which followed World War II. This renewal, which stimulated greater flexibility and more supple reflection in the missionary enterprise, marked a definite change. But it was only a matter of time that the Church in the Third World would 'come of age' and, in its quest for greater authenticity, would reject both the policy and the practice of missionary adaptation. While the renewal effort was undoubtedly a good one, it was too little too late. The end of the modern missionary era was already at hand.

CONCLUSION

1. If our above analysis is accepted, then the tendency to absolutise was most deeply ingrained and pervasive in that particular missionary spirit that began to develop in the sixteenth century and that culminated in the early and middle years of the present century. In both theory and practice, the missionary enterprise was imbued with the imperialist Christian assumption that Western Christianity was the only true expression of the Christian spirit, and hence *the* synthesis which had to be accepted as obligatory, necessary and indispensable for salvation. Since the forms of Western culture had been inspired and indeed consecrated by the Christian ideal, they were regarded as possessing universal validity.

2. The misguided pretensions to the absolute which we have described did not originate from any particular gospel imperative or divine commission. It is true, of course, that the Church has always regarded its missionary activity as a faithful response to Jesus' great commission to 'teach all nations'. Not to preach one's faith to others would be to commit the most serious failing of disobedience to Christ. Thus one of the constant, motivational forces in every missionary era has been the 'obedience-to-a-divine-call' motive—a motive, it should be added, that is sufficient unto itself to mobilise all manner of missionary forces. However, it was not this basic Christian motivation that gave rise to the unwarranted missionary pretensions to the absolute, but those 'extraneous motives', as Christopher Dawson called them, that take their rise in unconscious social conflicts at the historical level. Indeed the missionary tendency to absolutise was largely determined by forces that were not religious at all. The intrusion of these extraneous motives narrowed the whole missionary approach so as to exclude virtually any possibility of a genuinely *new* missionary outlook and strategy. There was only one way of being a good missionary—and no other.

3. All this, one might say, is ancient history. With the passing of the colonial era, the decline of Western prestige, the emergence of the Third World as a global power bloc, the new focus upon the function of the Church as sign rather than sanctuary, as missionary in its very nature and

not just in terms of its geographical expansion—with all this, and given our new historical consciousness, the danger of contemporary and future manifestations of this kind of absolutism in the missionary enterprise is perhaps minimal. Yet the blot that it places on the history of Christian missions and the toll that it has taken on the credibility of the Church justifies the effort to ask why such developments were possible. A Church that claims to be essentially missionary cannot move towards a new beginning until it has faced all the abuses and mistakes of the past with absolute honesty.

Christopher Mooney

The Claim of the Church to be Guardian of a Universal Natural and Moral Law

THE CONCEPT of a universal natural law has perhaps been the single most important element in the traditional Roman Catholic understanding of morality. The Church's claim to teach such universal morality, however, is today facing severe challenge. Indeed, there is hardly a more significant development in the post-conciliar Church than the decline of its authority in this area. To understand this phenomenon we shall first have to look briefly at the phenomenon of natural law itself. Then the Catholic Church's claim to be its guardian will appear in clearer perspective, and we shall be better able to judge this claim's current validity.

1

It is important to note at the outset that there is not one natural law tradition but many, with little more than verbal continuity between them. Needless to say, we are not here concerned with physical natural law, law as uniformity (like gravity, which cannot be disputed nor freely transgressed), but with moral natural law, law as norm of conduct. Medieval and modern conceptions of this moral natural law are really different doctrines altogether. Yet it is the medieval concept alone which has entered into traditional Roman Catholic teaching; the Church has given very little attention to those ideas of natural law which energised the American and French revolutions, much less to concepts developed in the writings of twentieth-century philosophers. This medieval tradition, however, was itself a synthesis. The Schoolmen, and especially Thomas Aquinas, wove together two main threads from the classical authors, the idea that natural law represented a higher ideal of justice in society, and the very different idea that it represented an animal instinct and a physical structure.

Cicero wrote eloquently of natural law in the first sense as 'right reason in agreement with nature, of universal application, unchanging and everlasting. . . . There will not be a different law at Rome and at Athens, a different law now and in the future, but one eternal and unchangeable law for all nations and for all times'.[1] This ideal goes back to the *Antigone* of Sophocles, the notion of an eternal and immutable justice, which human authority ought to express but frequently does not. Natural law in the second sense of animal instinct seems to have begun with the definition of Ulpian, a third-century lawyer, whose writings constituted almost a third of the *Code of Justinian*. 'Natural law indeed is not peculiar to the human race, but belongs to all animals.'[2] This outlook tends to judge what humans should do by seeing what animals do. It tends to focus upon the physical and biological structure of acts as the source of morality, especially sexual morality, and to shift perspective away from the moral questions with less 'physicality', such as economic justice and the norms for judging the rectitude of civil law.

Aquinas managed to combine these two threads. He understood natural law as a call to human beings to participate intellectually and actively in the eternal law, that rational ordering of the universe by a provident God. 'Among all others, the rational creature is subject to divine providence in a more excellent way, in so far as it itself partakes of a share of providence by being provident both for itself and others. Therefore it has a share of the eternal reason, whereby it has a natural inclination to its proper act and end; and this participation of the eternal law in the rational creature is called the 'natural law'.[3] More concretely, natural law is that inclination in all human beings to know and seek what is good for themselves, and to live in society according to this knowledge through the enactment of just civil law. But, precisely as animals, human beings also have all those inclinations which animals have generally, and so these too must pertain to natural law. Unlike animals, however, human beings consciously reflect upon this second set of inclinations and subject them to rational control.[4] They are thus not to be identified with natural law (though they might be called a law of nature); natural law is rather their recognition and the reasoned insight into how they should be followed in a given case.

This medieval effort was so valuable at the time because it opened up the possibility of giving a rational explanation for moral imperatives, an ethic based upon human existence as experienced, independently of any divine revelation. Aquinas wanted to establish some rational standard by which social and political institutions could be judged, a court of appeal, as it were, for the rejection of unjust laws. His natural law theory served importantly as a safeguard against government abuses, against the tyrannical assertion that human law was the pure command of the ruler. It was therefore a theory of what makes 'laws' laws, what gives them obligatory force. Only in a most secondary sense was its function to be that of positive civil law, namely to give explicit directives, since those directives which Aquinas believed were known clearly to everyone are of such a general character as seldom to give specific guidance regarding concrete decisions. Indeed his first formal principle of natural law (good is to be done and evil avoided) as well as its primary areas of material specification (the inclination to preservation of life, generation and education of offspring, organisation of society) were meant to focus less upon their content than upon the obligatory force somehow inherent in them, which is indeed universal and immutable: something should be done to preserve life, to organise the family and to stabilise society. In the concrete, this 'somehow' and this 'something' had to be derived from experience and enquiry by way of conclusion from these general principles. 'What pertains to moral science', said Aquinas, 'is known mostly through experience'.[5]

From such an emphasis upon experience it followed that exceptions, disagreements and the danger of making mistakes increase the more detailed these conclusions become. Whatever natural law may in fact demand in a concrete circumstance, therefore, need not be either rigidly applied universally nor clearly recognised by everyone who acts rationally.[6] For once one descends from first principles, the task of drawing detailed conclusions is simply too difficult, not only because of the innate weakness of human intelligence, but also because of the clouding of our self-knowledge by habit, prejudice, ignorance, and passion. Prudent estimates are the most we can expect in the majority of situations. Yet as responsible persons we must use what knowledge we have to shape our lives as best we can. This effort is all the more difficult in so far as we are continually confronted in the modern world with totally new situations. The human species has been developing over many centuries, and its maturity is evident today. We have only to think of the sophisticated dilemmas we must now face in bioethics to be aware of our constant need to draw from general principles ever new conclusions, unknown and unsought by former generations. Earlier conclusions may even need to be modified in these changed circumstances or discarded altogether as having no further application. Aquinas easily allowed for such change in conclusions from general principle, since he clearly believed that our knowledge of natural law can change and that human nature itself is not wholly immutable, something his interpreters have only recently been willing to admit.[7]

What then is the value and function of this medieval theory of natural law? On the social level, the most we can say is that it provides us with a criterion, a rational structure, whereby good laws may be seen to be good laws. As one authority has put it, 'It represents a pattern of law as law, discoverable, as patterns are, by those who enquire diligently; it might even be described as the special logic of law, as ever present and necessary to law as logic is to argument. . . . And as we may justify or invalidate an argument by appeal to logic, so we may justify or invalidate the laws of men by appeal to the natural law'.[8] On a more individual level, the 'nature' metaphor expresses that inner drive we all feel toward authentic personhood and self-realisation, a tendency rather than a code, 'a dynamically inviting possibility, a concrete project to be carried out in the midst of a concrete situation'.[9] On both these levels moral striving is a constant, but its constancy is not that of a law in a legalistic or static sense, but that of an inbuilt directedness toward one's end. This dynamic bent in human persons, according to Aquinas, is perceived by practical reason on the conscious level in the form of moral imperatives, which in turn become the actions constituting the concrete conclusions of natural law.[10]

2

The primary purpose for the development of this medieval theory of natural law was, as we said, to establish some order in the political and social institutions of Western Europe. Those who suffered from predatory overlords had to be given guidance and protection, and the Church tried to do both. Rarely, however, was natural law ever mentioned in the official teaching of Church documents. Rarer still were attempts to ground in natural law theory those centuries-old prohibitions against fornication, divorce, birth control or abortion. All these prohibitions were presumed to be clearly present in Sacred Scripture and were so presented to the faithful long before the medieval synthesis.[11] Only in the last century, when Leo XIII chose Thomistic philosophy as the model for Catholic schools, did Catholic moralists begin seriously to highlight natural law theory as the warrant for specific moral teaching.

Leo himself was indeed very close to Aquinas' original concerns when he treated questions of social morality from a natural law perspective: the right to private property and a just wage, the right of workers to organise, etc. Pius XI followed this same general approach when commenting on national socialism in Germany, for example, as well as on the rights of parents to educate children, and on labour-management relations in *Quadragesimo Anno*. The public treatises of Pius XII did the same in seeking to ground upon a natural moral order the great political, social and international issues of his long pontificate. In *Pacem in Terris* John XXIII could address his discussions of rights to all persons of good will, not just to Christians, because he emphasised that freedom and intelligence are images of the divine in all men and women, and that human reason is therefore capable of discovering these demands of human dignity placed in creatures by the Creator.

In none of these papal documents, however, was there any effort to deduce detailed conclusions from the first principles of natural law. The emphasis was consistently upon a very general recognition of the rights of persons through appeal to legal philosophy, anthropology and data from the social sciences, an approach accepted by many who would never susbcribe to the scholastic understanding of natural law. The popes' claim was that all reasonable people should be able to discern a human right to minimum levels of food, clothing and shelter, the values of work and family, the binding nature of contracts, as well as the need for both freedom and interdependence. At the same time there was also a claim, quite consistent with natural law theory, that Christian faith can make a significant contribution to social morality, because in fact these moral insights of reasonable people correspond with traditional Christian values and teaching. All these documents speak of 'reason enlightened by revelation'. Coherence between these two claims has indeed been one of the basic methodological principles of the popes' pronouncements on social morality.[12]

The Church's competence to interpret natural moral law regarding social justice thus appears presented as clearly a negative competence: reason cannot contradict any of the ethical principles of fundamental Christian doctrine. The task of the Church is to shape certain patterns of thinking which follow from this revealed doctrine and then to use these patterns as a check upon movements in society with potential to damage human life. Such 'critical negativity', to use Edward Schillebeeckx's phrase, is a positive power exercising constant pressure to bring about what is most desirable for society, not by explicit detailed formulations, but by negative knowledge. For in strictly human and secular concerns the Church has as little positive idea as non-believers of what is most worthy of the human person. Popes must consider various alternatives, keeping in mind, as they search, human values already realised in history. If in their encyclicals they protest against certain public situations or goals, they do so in the name of values still being sought by humankind and contained negatively in Christian revelation, in the contrast experience of what is unworthy of human dignity.

This does not mean, of course, that the Church cannot condemn a very specific social evil as an affront to the human person. In the agrarian world of the Middle Ages, for example, the prevailing forms of usury were clearly harmful. Everyone agrees now that it was wise for the Church to prohibit interest on loans at that time, in a culture where all loans were agricultural and where the exploited were always poor peasants dependent upon changing weather. It was a mistake, however, to have been seduced by circumstances of a particular time and place into thinking and declaring an expedient economic policy to be an immutable truth of Christian morals, simply because it was a conclusion reasonable persons could then deduce from the first principles of natural law. For centuries the Church proclaimed this prohibition as unchangeable doctrine. As Europe moved into the new commercial civilisation of the Renaissance, the force of Church authority thus prevented good loans as well as bad. Aquinas' insistence on the time-bound nature of all conclusions from natural law principles could have avoided this. 'Practical reason', he had said, 'being concerned with human conduct, has to do with the contingent. And so, though there is a certain necessity about its general principles, the further it descends into detail, the more it may encounter exceptions. . . . In the practical order there is not the same truth or practical rightness for everybody, as far as detail is concerned, but only in general principles. . . .'[13]

In economic and social matters the Church has never made the usury mistake again. When it has appealed to natural law in these areas it has been careful not to descend into this kind of detail, and it has also tended to understand 'natural' in more general terms, as that which belongs to the basic structures of human life recognised by all rational persons. Since the appearance of that very important document of Vatican II, *Gaudium et Spes, the Pastoral Constitution on the Church in the Modern World,* the Church's epistemological claim in regard to natural law seems to have become more modest still, more cautious and more nuanced. Roman Catholicism now recognises more readily the intellectual and cultural pluralism which exists in modern society and no longer claims privileged insight into concrete conclusions about social obligation, unless these are explicitly related to Christian revelation. Recent documents do not hide the fact that they are proceeding on the basis of non-universal form of moral reasoning, and whatever certitudes they proclaim have a much more distinctly Christian basis. These documents more easily accept the inevitability of conflict on the philosophical level as well as on the level of politics and social life, and are content with conclusions on these levels which are ambiguous, partial and incomplete.[14]

3

This recent approach to natural law in dealing with social morality contrasts strongly with the approach in documents dealing with sexual morality. In the social area, as we saw, the Church has claimed a negative competence to reject ethical positions that contradict statements in revelation about human life. It has also claimed a positive competence to propose moral norms already embraced by the world community and in keeping with its aspirations for justice. But the Church has avoided specifying these norms in detail. It has advocated a just wage for workers, for example, as something in accord with natural law, but it has not used its teaching authority to state what such a wage should be in the concrete (other than that it should provide adequately for the needs of the worker and his family), since circumstances of time and place would introduce serious disagreements and elicit very diverse opinions. This does not mean that the Church does not have the authority, if it so wishes, to propose very detailed norms for social morality which are established neither through revelation nor through common human consciousness. But then it would clearly be in the area of contingent human knowledge. Before it did this, dialogue with the larger human community would be absolutely essential for credibility, and any claim that the norms in question were grounded in natural law would have to be supported by serious reasons and argument.

Yet in the area of sexual morality papal documents have consistently proposed just such detailed norms, and have consistently claimed that these norms are to be found in the natural law. Indeed, natural law theory seems to have been viewed over the last century as a refuge against the changing sexual mores of a secular world, a bastion within which moral precepts could be taught with certitude and any violations condemned by absolute prohibition. In *Humanae Vitae,* to take the latest and clearest example, Paul VI was not simply content to reaffirm as a fundamental principle the inseparable unity between love and fecundity in human sexuality, an ideal which would find broad acceptance in the human community. The whole point of the encyclical was rather that this principle must apply to each individual sexual act in marriage: every marriage act must remain open to the transmission of life; there is an inseparable link between its procreative and unitive meanings. While it is permissible directly to contravene this imperative by systematic abstinence during the fertile periods, any artifical contraceptive procedures are intrinsically evil.[15] Pope Paul made no attempt to support this central conclusion from Scripture, nor did he make much of an argument from tradition, citing references to documents going no further back than the last century. He noted that the teaching has been constantly proposed by tradition, but this obviously argued not for its truth but for its longevity. Its truth and certitude, he insisted, come from its firm grounding in the natural moral law.

Why this insistence on such clarity of detail in the natural law regarding sexual morality? The reason is that Catholic moralists of the past, when dealing with sexual matters, opted for a biological concept of nature in the rigid mode of Ulpian, which, as we noted earlier, represented one strand only of the natural law tradition incorporated into the medieval synthesis. They also committed themselves to an obsolete biology, by continuing to attribute a meaning to all sexual acts on the basis of what is now known to happen with relative rarity. This approach is clearly out of touch with much contemporary theological thought, as well as with the whole thrust of the *Pastoral Constitution on the Church in the Modern World,* which sees the human person, not the operations of some isolated human organ, as the fundamental moral criterion for human actions.[16] In other words, biological fertility has to get its moral meaning from its ordination towards those goods which define the total institution of marriage. Pope Paul did not deny that purposes other than biological finality are involved in marital sexuality (a clear advance over Ulpian and the medievalists), but these can be tolerated, he said, only as long as the 'nature of the act' is respected (a regression from Vatican II's emphasis on the 'nature of the person').[17]

Such an understanding of natural law as identical with natural physical processes is obviously more applicable to sexual than to social matters, and this explains the ease with which the Church has been able to descend into such detail when speaking of sex. But the consequences can be embarrassing, as *Humanae Vitae* proved, for nowhere in the encyclical was the central conclusion shown as following reasonably from a widely accepted general moral principle. The conclusion was simply asserted without supporting argument. This would, of course, be understandable in a document explaining divine revelation. But since neither revelation nor infallibility were involved here, the degree of Church authority behind the teaching remained unjustified, and the responsibility to supply reasons correspondingly more urgent. This was all the more imperative because the conclusion was supposed to derive exclusively from natural law, whose obligatory force is constituted precisely by human reasoning. Not to supply a reasoned argument was therefore to raise the suspicion that none exists. Simply to *declare* that artificial contraception is intrinsically evil was to use Church authority to deprive natural law in this case of its whole epistemological base and to turn it into a purely juridical concept.[18] It was also to confuse the teaching office of the Church with its governing office, since the encyclical's authoritative teaching on natural law inevitably assumed a purely disciplinary connotation that concerned Catholics alone.

The generally strong negative reaction to *Humanae Vitae* as contrary to the lived experience of both Catholics and persons of other faiths raises a host of ecclesiological problems regarding the exercise of the Church's non-infallible teaching authority. How precisely ought this teaching deal with issues of natural law so as to function in more than a juridical way? Is the pope's particular teaching office to be identified with its monarchical expression? Pope Paul appealed to 'the light of the Holy Spirit' to substantiate his position on contraception. But does such an appeal imply a power somehow to achieve outside the human process a truth which is in principle accessible to all reasonable persons? Does moral persuasiveness require identifying the various processes within which the Spirit is presumed to be operating? Does it also require a broad consultation at all levels of Church life, and a listening to this collaborative effort before putting full papal authority behind the assertion that a highly disputed concrete moral norm enjoys the status of a natural law?[19]

Once again, however, as in the case of social morality, the issue is not whether the Church should propose moral norms. It should. But when these are established neither through revelation nor through a general consensus of the human community, then prior dialogue with this community is essential for credibility, and the norms themselves should be imposed upon the Catholic conscience only to the extent that valid reasons can be found to ground them in natural law. The more concrete and detailed these norms are, the more imperative this mode of procedure becomes. This is the way for the Church to be truly prophetic, as it surely was in the great social encyclicals of the present century. This is how it can truly fulfil its vocation to be the living conscience of the world. Nor should it hesitate to use natural law as a vehicle for its pedagogy, as long as it is faithful to the full range of its own natural law tradition. For that tradition is not based on commands and prohibitions so much as upon human potentiality and rational discussion, and as such it offers a genuine framework for universal public morality.

Notes

1. Cicero *De Republica* book III, §33; Sophocles *Antigone* lines 450 ff. See the magisterial study of O. Lottin *Le Droit naturel chez Saint Thomas d'Aquin et ses prédécesseurs,* 2nd ed. (Bruges 1931) and the briefer studies by A. P. D'Entrèves *Natural Law* (London 1970) and D. J. O'Connor *Aquinas and Natural Law* (London 1967).

2. Justinian *Digest* book I, tit. 1, lines 1 ff.

3. *Summa Theologica,* 1a. 2ae. Q. 91 art. 2. See also art. 1.

4. *ibid.,* Qg. 94 art. 2.

5. *In decem libros Ethicorum expositio,* book I, lec. 3, §38. See also *Summa Theologica,* 1a. 2ae. Q. 94, artt. 2 and 6. I have adopted here the insights of C. Ryan, 'The Traditional Concept of Natural Law: An Interpretation' in I. Evans ed., *Light on the Natural Law* (Baltimore 1965) pp. 18-19, 27-31.

6. *Summa Theologica,* 1a. 2ae. Q. 94, artt. 4 and 6; *De Malo,* Q. 2 artt. 4 and 13.

7. *Summa Theologica,* 1a. 2ae. Q. 94, art. 5; Supplement, Q. 41, artt. 1 and 3. Thomas' succinct principle, 'diversa diversis mensuris mensurantur', appears in 1a. 2ae. Q. 104, artt. 3 and 1. See J. Fuchs *Natural Law* (New York 1965) pp. 85-119.

8. Ryan, in the article cited in note 5.

9. L. Monden *Sin, Liberty and Law* (New York 1965) 89.

10 See *Summa Theologica,* 1a. 2ae. Q. 90, art. 1 and 2; Q. 94, art. 1 and 2.

11. As an example see J. T. Noonan, Jr. *Contraception: A History of its Treatment by the Catholic Theologians and Canonists* (Cambridge, U.S.A. 1965) pp. 57-106.

12. See the analysis of papal social teaching in D. Hollenbach *Claims in Conflict* (New York 1979) pp. 107-133.

13. *Summa Theologica,* 1a. 2ae. Q. 94, art. 4.

14. On these changes in outlook compare with earlier documents the following sections of *Gaudium et Spes:* §§10, 11, 22, 26, 41, 53 and 59. See also Hollenbach, cited in note 12.

15. *Humanae Vitae,* §§ 11, 12, 13 and 14.

16. The norm proposed in *Gaudium et Spes,* §51, is that the moral aspect of any procedure must be determined by objective standards 'based on the nature of the human person and his acts'. The Church's response at various stages in the history of sexual morality is fascinating and has been traced by several scholars. For example, Noonan *Contraception* (cited in note 11), Farley 'Sexual Ethics' *Encyclopedia of Bioethics* (New York 1978) IV pp. 1575-1589.

17. See *Humanae Vitae* §§ 10, 11, 13, 16 and 17. This shortcoming has been well addressed by J. A. Selling 'Moral Teaching, Traditional Teaching, and "Humanae Vitae"' *Louvain Stud.* 7 (1978) 24-44.

18. See J. A. Komonchak 'Humanae Vitae and its Reception: Ecclesiological Reflections' *Theological Studies* 39 (1978) 250-257.

19. A recent issue of *Chicago Studies* 17 (1978) 149-307 deals at length with these and similar questions.

PART II

Fundamental Approaches

Jost Eckert

The Gospel for Israel and the Nations: The Problem of the Absoluteness of Christianity in the New Testament

THE SENSE of missionary obligation to convert to the Christian faith all those of our fellow-men who do not believe in Jesus Christ, on the grounds that it is in Christ alone that salvation is to be found (Acts 4:11 f.), has been a characteristic mark of the Christian outlook from the earliest days of the history of Christianity right down to the present time. The word spoken by the Johannine Christ: 'I am the way, the truth and the life' (John 14:6), and the commission given by the risen Christ, the Lord of the Church, to his apostles: 'Go . . . and make disciples of all nations' (Matt. 28:19), form the basis of the claim that the gospel must be preached to all peoples as the decisive and unsurpassable saving truth.

This claim to 'absolute' truth is called into question by modern man. There are many different reasons for this. Not least among them is the way in which historical research (on which historical and critical exegesis recognises its dependence) has produced a sense of the relativity of all human and historical factors. The historical problem is: How unique is the Christian gospel? The theological problem is concerned with the question whether the Christian proclamation can be considered as necessary for salvation in view of the profusion of other faiths and religions. The problem of the absoluteness of Christianity has been brought into sharper relief by the new encounter with the faith of Israel and by the positive attitude to non-Christian religions commended by the Second

35

Vatican Council. In this context the chief task of New Testament exegesis is to explore the history of the gospel and seek to bring to light the way in which the first Christians understood their faith.

1. JESUS AND ISRAEL

The oft-quoted statement of Julius Wellhausen: 'Jesus was not a Christian but a Jew'[1] not only raises the theological problem as to whether Jesus and his message are to be understood as a purely Jewish phenomenon, but also obliges us to ask how far the Christian Church is permanently bound up with Israel, in view of the importance it attaches to continuity with the earthly Jesus and the fact that it proclaims such continuity in the gospels.

Though the texts of the gospels bear the stamp of the Christian faith, they leave no doubt about the basically pro-Israelite attitude of Jesus. Even though he had a great deal new to say to his contemporaries, with his announcement of the nearness of the Kingdom of God (Mark 1:15) and the consequences which followed from it, he proclaimed no new God, but rather the God of Israel revealed in a new way—the God who, according to the faith of Israel, was conceived of as the Lord of history and the Creator of the world and all men. The Gospel of Jesus was directed towards Israel, and when he did not find the expected response among his own people he did not abandon Israel and turn to the gentiles. The mission to the gentiles did not come within the field of vision of the earthly Jesus. Rather, Israel was and remained for him the centre of God's saving activity. This is in fact confirmed, assuming that we have here an authentic word of Jesus, by his prophetic-apocalyptic warning to his unrepentant contemporaries: 'I tell you, many will come from East and West and sit at table with Abraham, Isaac and Jacob in the kingdom of heaven, while the sons of the kingdom will be thrown into the outer darkness; there men will weep and gnash their teeth' (Matt. 8-11 f.; Luke 13:28 f.). It is not a question here of the mission to the gentiles, but of the coming together of the gentiles brought about by God, in accordance with the prophetic tradition concerning the eschatological pilgrimage of the nations.[2] The threat against the sons of the kingdom—by which are meant those Jews who have nothing to do with the message of Jesus concerning the Kingdom of God—does not imply that the election of Israel has been completely abandoned. On the contrary, it is expressly stated that the Israel of the patriarchs, to which Jesus recognises himself bound, along with all believers, is the foundation of the eschatological salvation-community.

As the formation of the group of twelve disciples shows, Jesus initiated a movement to gather the Israelites together and staked a permanent claim on them (see Matt. 19:28; Luke 22:28-30). When the Israel of his time showed itself to be largely closed to his message, he went to death for his people. Of course exegesis encounters some very difficult questions at this very point, since such texts as Mark 10:45 and 14:24 express first and foremost the Church's belief in the universal redemptive significance of the death of Jesus, and the question remains as to how far we can discover what Jesus thought of his own death. If however we bear in mind that Jesus, as he went to Jerusalem, must have had to reckon with the likelihood of his having to share the unhappy fate of the prophets, then we shall have to agree with H. Schürmann: 'Unless we want to assume that Jesus in dying suffered a moral breakdown, then we may suppose that he went to his death in love and offering himself for others.'[3] It goes without saying that those towards whom his activity had been directed up to that point, the Jewish people, were not excluded from the benefits of his death. If he interpreted his death in the light of the figure of the 'suffering servant of God' (Isa. 53:4-12), then a universal application of his sacrifice is implied, in the sense of a dying 'for many', that is to say for all sinners. In addition, the universal salvation-perspective of God's eschatological rule frequently breaks through in his preaching.

We must not overlook the fact that alongside the basic pro-Israelite attitude of Jesus, there are elements which are critical of Israel and which shatter any narrow belief in election. Putting it in rather an extreme way, Jesus was, from the religious and political points of view, no nationalist. He shared the prophetic critical view of John the Baptist, who said to the self-confident religious people of Israel: 'Bear fruits that befit repentance, and do not begin to say to yourselves, "We have Abraham as our father"; for I tell you, God is able from these stones to raise up children to Abraham' (Luke 3:8; Matt. 3:8 f.). It is not being a descendant of Abraham in a racial sense that guarantees entry into the Kingdom of God; what is decisive is the faith which produces the fruits of repentance. So Jesus does nothing expressly to revive the national hopes of Israel, and he puts forward no political theology along the lines of the Zealots. He does not call people to a holy war against Rome. The conditions of salvation are personalised—that is to say, the subject of his teaching is the individual in his personal relationship with God and with his neighbour (see the parables and the ethical teaching of Jesus).

There can be a crossing of dogmatic frontiers, as may be seen in the encounters of Jesus with the pagan centurion of Capernaum (Luke 7:1-10; Matt. 8:5-13) and the Canaanitish woman (Mark 7:24-30; Matt. 15:21-28). The faith of these pagans, who put the faith of the Israelites to shame, is the pre-condition of the experience of salvation. Yahweh is understood, more strongly than in the faith of Israel, as the father of all men.

The parable of the Good Samaritan (Luke 10:29-37) presents the behaviour of one who was despised in Israel as an example to be followed. Considered in the context of the message of Jesus, the Samaritan's behaviour is morally appropriate to the rule of God. Since it is not suggested that such a principle of conduct was known to him, he has been regarded as an example of the 'anonymous' Christian. In the parable of the final judgment (Matt. 25:31-46), Christian tradition took this universal element in the message of Jesus—that salvation can be found outside an explicit relationship to Christ and the Church—and gave it wider expression in a radical and impressive way that has never been surpassed.

Jesus himself lived out this unrestricted brotherliness, caring particularly for those who in Israel were the object of religious and social discrimination. The parable about the father who accepts and the brother who rejects (Luke 15:11-32) not only demonstrates that Jesus was opposed to the exclusive way in which the religious people in Israel understood salvation, with their rejection of sinners, but also indicates the new image of God that Jesus presents. The particularism of the Jewish view of salvation was called into question by the universal dimension of the Kingdom of God as it was proclaimed by Jesus, who mediated God's saving rule to men and offered salvation to the poor, the hungry and the weeping (Luke 6:20b-21). This universal dimension receives material confirmation and support from his belief in God as the Father. There is no trace of the thought of a 'holy remnant', as a group of the elect, in the message of Jesus,[4] and there is no reference to Israel in the Lord's Prayer.[5]

The conviction that God's compassion is greater than his justice, and that he desires men's salvation, is reflected also in Jesus' much-discussed criticism of the law. At all events the Torah is for him no longer a sacrosanct standard. He preaches the will of God in a new way which implies criticism of the law (see, e.g., Mark 2:27; 7:15; 10:11 f.). His ethical teaching shows that the ideal of the totally other world of the Kingdom of God must be the decisive factor. The life of Jesus himself makes it clear that this is already a source of power for anyone who believes.[6] What Jesus called into question was not so much Israel's beliefs about salvation-history as its beliefs about the law.

Christian faith sees in Jesus the one 'anointed by the Spirit' (see Luke 4:16-30), who in a unique way brought God as a saving reality within the experience of those who were open to him. This is the greatest miracle of his life, and together with his resurrection marks the beginning of the *basileia*. Jewish faith was not, however, ready to recognise this inbreaking of redemption through the life, activity and destiny of Jesus of Nazareth.

2. THE CHRISTIAN GOSPEL AND ISRAEL

After Easter, the disciples of Jesus continued to preach in Israel the Gospel of Jesus, and they proclaimed Jesus himself as the one who through the resurrection had been confirmed as Israel's Messiah, and who would soon come again in judgment as the Son of Man and make the Kingdom of God visible to all the world.

The outward course of the history of the relationship between the followers of Jesus and official Judaism is, with all its uncertainties, easier to sketch in detail than the development of Christian theology in the first twenty-five years. The sources present difficult problems, and hypothetical judgments are unavoidable. There is no doubt, however, that the division produced in Israel by the critical preaching of Jesus, and by his death, took its course, and that in the decades which followed the two sides came to be more clearly differentiated. For Jewish Christians, Jesus was the decisive figure who mediated salvation, who put all other salvation-figures in the shade, and who could be described by all the relevant titles salvation-history could provide. Since Jesus was understood from now on as the incarnate Word of God and the final authority, the Torah, even for Jewish Christians who were loyal to it, had to be regarded increasingly as relative. While in Judaism the Torah—as it had already been in pre-Christian times—was identified with the divine Wisdom, and its pre-existence and involvement as mediator in the work of creation were proclaimed (see Ecclus. 24; Wisd. of Sol. 9:9; Prov. 3:19; 8:22), on the Christian side the development proceeded in precisely the opposite direction: the recognition of the meaning of Jesus for salvation increases, and the significance of the *torāh* decreases. In Christian worship there is introduced, alongside the service of the Word, the remembrance of the saving death of Jesus by which the new covenant was inaugurated.

The universalism of the message of Jesus, and the fact that his vicarious, expiatory death called in question both temple and law (see 1 Cor. 15:3; Rom. 3:25; Acts 7) seems to have been more clearly recognised and more provocatively proclaimed by Greek-speaking Jewish Christians living in Jerusalem than by the Galilean disciples of Jesus or the Aramaic-speaking Jerusalem Christians. If the death of Stephen and the expulsion of the Hellenists (Acts 7:54; 8:3) was the outward reason why the gospel came out across the frontiers of Israel, it was not entirely fortuitous, but corresponded to the inner dynamic of the gospel, that in Antioch it led to preaching to the gentiles and the establishment of a Church composed of Jews and gentiles (Acts 11:19-26). The abandonment of circumcision, the basic Jewish sacrament by which proselytes were incorporated into the covenant with Abraham (see Gen. 17), could

D

only be risked as the result of a creative interpretation of the gospel. It is understandable that the timid conservatism of the Jewish Christians should have protested against this development (see Gal. 2:4; Acts 15; Matt. 10:5 f.).

It must be admitted that the expulsion of the Hellenists and the rejection of the gospel from the Jewish side encouraged the turning to the gentiles, and that, further, with the subsequent endorsement by the so-called Apostolic Council[7] of the abandonment of circumcision for gentile Christians, external facts of history led to the creation of theology—according to Gal. 2:7-9 the success of the mission was a criterion for recognising that the mission to the gentiles should be free from the law. The thought that the events of history can be understood as God-directed salvation-history should not, however, have been strange to Israel.

Of course it is part of the tragedy of Christian-Jewish history—and how else can one describe it?—that Jewish Christianity was increasingly overtaken by gentile Christianity, that for various reasons it became a historical backwater, and that it finally disappeared from Church history—not least because of the catastrophe of A.D. 70 and its aftermath. In consequence the close relationship of Christianity with the Israel of the patriarchs and with the Jewish people—a relationship which had found its clearest expression in Jewish Christianity—was greatly diminished, and it came to be largely forgotten that, for Christians in the tradition of Jesus and the apostles, Israel had been the first partner in dialogue and, as the regular object of Christian preaching, had continued to be constantly challenged by the Christian mission. A Christian Church which neglects this aspect of its gospel, denies its origin and its apostolic history.

The theological conception that the Christian Church is the faithful and true Israel, which has simply taken the place of the Israel which has rejected Jesus, is too simple and is not supported by the evidence of the New Testament as a whole. It is true that the earliest Christian community in Jerusalem saw itself as the eschatological salvation-community and as faithful Israel, but the judgment on Israel for not believing in Jesus as the Messiah does not seem to have been at all clear from the beginning.

It is well known that Paul himself, the missionary to the gentiles, who could be very severe on Israel for not believing in Jesus (see Gal. 3 and 4; Rom. 9:6 ff.; 11:7 ff., 17, 21) and who saw Christianity as the faithful Remnant preserving the continuity of salvation-history (Rom. 11:1-10), nevertheless believed firmly in the place of 'all Israel' in salvation-history, and warned the gentile Christians against arrogance. Even Israel which does not believe in Jesus remains potentially the salvation-community: 'A hardening has come upon part of Israel, until the full number of the gentiles come in, and so all Israel will be saved; as it is written. . . .' (Rom.

11:25c-26). We should not be too ready to dismiss this belief of the apostle as apocalyptic day-dreaming, since he is here concerned with the whole problem of God's justice and his truthfulness in the light of his promises to Israel.[8]

In their own individual ways, Luke and Matthew in their writings very clearly present the Church composed of Jews and Gentiles as Israel's successor in the unfolding of salvation-history, and they do not seem to share Paul's hope for the conversion of Israel. However, it is doubtful whether they would claim that with the quotations from Isaiah about 'hardening' (Acts 28:26 f. and Matt. 13:14 f.) and other prophecies of doom (see Acts 3:13; Matt. 21:43), God's last word on unbelieving Israel had been spoken.[9] Christian preaching cannot anticipate God's final judgments, as the lack of uniformity in the New Testament sayings on judgment demonstrates.

3. JESUS CHRIST—'LIGHT TO LIGHTEN THE GENTILES'

The extent to which, from the point of view of salvation-history, the preaching of the gospel to the Gentiles has its origin in Israel, is made clear by the gentile Christian Luke in the Song of Simeon: 'Lord, now lettest thou thy servant depart in peace, according to thy word; for mine eyes have seen thy salvation which thou hast prepared in the presence of all peoples, a light for revelation to the gentiles, and for glory to thy people Israel' (Luke 2:29-32). From a Christian point of view, the promise concerning the Servant of God, who was appointed to be 'a covenant to the people (Israel), a light to the nations (gentiles)' (Isa. 42:6; see 49:6[10]), has found its fulfilment in Jesus Christ. The light for the nations is not Israel, which refuses its allegiance to Jesus and his gospel (see also Luke 2:34), but Jesus Christ is the messenger and mediator of salvation. He is more than Israel's Messiah; he is the new Adam (see 1 Cor. 15:45; Rom. 5:12-21; Luke 3:23-38).

We have already said that the close relationship of salvation-history with Israel is more strongly emphasised by Paul, who more than any other was responsible for the founding and promotion, historically, of the mission to the gentiles, than it is later by Luke. The gospel which is preached to the gentiles is basically a Jewish-Christian one. Christian missionary preaching does not proclaim the God of pagan religions or philosophers, but the God who has revealed himself in the history of Israel and in Jesus Christ. The Old Testament scriptures are retained as sources of revelation, and interpreted in the light of Christ. The salvation-history thought-categories of the Old Testament are normative for the language of New Testament theology (see, for example, the conception of promise and fulfilment, old and new covenants, the profusion of christological titles, the expectation of judgment and of the Kingdom of God, and above all the eschatological way of thinking, as opposed to non-historical cyclical concepts). This connection with salvation-history saved the Christ-kerygma from degenerating into myth.

Paul is stating the fundamentals of the gospel as it is preached to the gentiles when in 1 Thess. 1:9 f., he reminds the Thessalonians that they have 'turned to God from idols, to serve a living and true God, and to wait for his Son from heaven, whom he raised from the dead, Jesus who delivers us from the wrath to come'. When belief in the wrath of the gods disappears, the gods themselves are no longer taken seriously. The Christian message of good news and the Pauline preaching of grace do not imply the abandonment of the idea of judgment, but rather the promise of deliverance for all those who let themselves be grasped by Jesus Christ and the reconciliation-event which God has offered in him (see Rom. 5:9; 2 Cor. 5:18-21). This salvation is offered to all, without exception; therefore 'in Christ' all religious, national, social and sexual differences are abolished (see Gal. 3:28; 1 Cor. 12:13; Eph. 2:11-21).

It is a basic presupposition of the New Testament that, when faced with the gospel, men find themselves in a situation which calls for decision. However, the problem of the lack of openness of both Jews and Gentiles is strongly felt, and—though there is no suggestion that they are not guilty—the fact that unbelievers are blind and held captive is recognised: 'and even if our gospel is veiled, it is veiled only to those who are perishing. In their case the god of this world has blinded the minds of the unbelievers, to keep them from seeing the light of the gospel of the glory of Christ, who is the likeness of God' (2 Cor. 4:3 f; see 3:14 f. and the passages on predestination in Rome; 8:28-30; 9:11-29; John 8:34 f.; but see also Acts 3:17).

The preaching of the gospel, which evokes both acceptance and rejection, salvation and disaster (2 Cor. 2:14-16), leads, according to Paul, not only to a purifying self-knowledge on the part of the Jews (see Phil. 3:7-11; Rom. 10:2 f.), but also to the recognition of unbelief and false belief among the gentiles. It is only in the light of the gospel—this is how Rom. 1:18—3:20 is to be interpreted—that the full extent of the godlessness and lost condition of man in the grip of sin can be known. In Rom. 1:18-32 Paul does not simply take a positive view of the gentiles' natural knowledge of God; rather, he accuses them of not holding fast to 'what can be known about God', 'his eternal power and deity', which can be 'clearly perceived in the things that have been made' (vv. 19 f.), and of not letting it issue in a real recognition of God, but rather relapsing into the worship of idols (see Gal. 4:8). Therefore their hearts and their intellects have been plunged into darkness, and those who rejected God have been themselves abandoned by God. They have lost their bearings, and have fallen into the salvationless state of a perverted order of creation.

We must not overlook the fact that this, like other statements of Paul, is exaggerated for polemical purposes. He paints such a uniformly gloomy picture of heathenism in order to make the light of the gospel shine correspondingly more brightly. It is also noteworthy that the grounds on which he accuses the gentiles imply also an admission that in some degree they are on the way to a right knowledge of God. He does not speak of a total blindness to God and his will. It is in conformity with this, that Paul concedes in Rom. 2:14 f. not only that the gentiles' conscience accuses them rightly, but also that they—and Paul again speaks without qualification—'do by instinct what the law commands' (= the ethical teaching of the Torah).

Luke, who as a Christian writer deliberately seeks to enter into dialogue with the Hellenistic world, allows his Paul in Athens to declare himself against the worship of idols (Acts 17:16, 24 f., 29), but Paul's speech to the Areopagus, as Luke presents it (Acts 17:22-31),[11] has, by comparison with Rom. 1, a much stronger tendency to establish contact than to oppose. Since this is the only sermon of Paul to a gentile audience recorded by Luke it has a representative character and brings out the desire for a positive evaluation of gentile religion and philosophy. Paul testifies here to the Athenians that they are 'religious' (v. 22), and that in worshipping the 'unknown God' they are searching for the true God (v. 23). He is the one whom the gospel can reveal as the creator of the world and of all men, as the goal of all men's quest for salvation, and as the God of salvation-history.

SUMMARY AND OUTLOOK

According to the New Testament, the Christian faith is the gospel for Israel and the nations. At the centre of the kerygma is Jesus Christ, who in an unsurpassable and definitive way has brought God near to man as saving reality. The Church has the task of proclaiming this good news of reconciliation, that in Christ the new creation breaks in (2 Cor. 5:14-21) and the world finds its unity, its deliverance and its fulfilment.[12]

The historical gospel does not express 'absolute' truths, but seeks to bring home to men, in all its richness of meaning, God's Word, which in Jesus has become flesh (John 1:14). It can, however, never be fully grasped. Since God has spoken 'through a human being in a human way',[13] the historical situation of the gospel at any given time must be taken into account. The early Christian preaching aimed at the Jews was specially characterised by opposition and separation; what Jews and Christians had in common often disappeared into the background. Paul, particularly in his theology of the cross, presents the gospel as a criticism of both Jewish and pagan religion, where as Luke evaluates Greek religion and philosophy more positively and proclaims Jesus Christ and the gospel more emphatically as the answer to the human longing for salvation. The dualism so prominent in John's Gospel between believers in Jesus and the unbelieving world, reflects the situation in the Johannine community, which, set in an environment often openly hostile to the gospel and faced with disorders within the Church, is intent on the consolidation of the brotherly community of disciples and directs its gaze on Jesus Christ with an unparalleled degree of christological concentration. The first letter of Peter also has this separation, resulting from a similar situation and pastoral necessity, and this gives rise at the same time to the thought of election on the part of Christians who feel themselves to be strangers in the world.[14] Such situations did not, however, cause the New Testament Church to abandon its mission. Rather, the gospel forced believers to give an account of their hope (1 Pet. 3:15) and to proclaim God as the one 'who wants everyone to be saved' (1 Tim. 2:4; see John 3:16 f.; 17:18). The Church of the New Testament can speak of God's will for universal salvation in an optimistic way which almost demolishes its own doctrinal structure (see also Rom. 11:32; Heb. 11:6), because it knows that God is not to be limited or held down.

The many-sided, often daring, re-interpretation of the one gospel in the early days of Christianity raises for us the question as to whether the significance of Jesus Christ for salvation has ever been presented to people of other historical situations, and other religions and cultures, in a manner adequate to their needs.

Translated by G. W. S. Knowles

Notes

1. J. Wellhausen *Einleitung in die drei ersten Evangelien* (Berlin 1905) p. 113.

2. See Isa. 2:1-4; 25:6-8; Mic. 4:1; Zech. 2:11.

3. H. Schürmann 'Wie hat Jesus seinen Tod bestanden und verstanden' in *Orientierung an Jesus/Zur Theologie der Synoptiker, für J. Schmid* ed. P. Hoffmann (Freiburg i.B. 1973) pp. 325-363; and p. 348. See also K. Kertelge, ed. *Der Tod Jesu/Deutungen im NT* (Freiburg i.B. 1976).

4. Mark 13:20, 23, 27 par. and Luke 18:7 are texts of an apocalyptic character and possible secondary.

5. See G. Lohfink 'Universalismus und Exklusivität des Heils im NT' in *Absolutheit des Christentums* ed. W. Kasper (Freiburg i.B. 1977) pp. 63-82; and p. 73.

6. See J. Eckert 'Wesen und Funktion der Radikalismen in der Botschaft Jesu' *Münchener Theol. Zeitschrift 24* (1973) 301-325.

7. See J. Eckert 'Paulus und die Jerusalemer Autoritäten nach dem Galater-brief und der Apostelgeschichte' *Schriftauslegung* ed. J. Ernst (Paderborn 1972) 281-311.

8. See J. Eckert 'Paulus und Israel' *Trierer Theol. Zwitschr. 87* (1978) 1-13.

9. For information on the very different assessments of Luke's understanding of Israel, see P.-G. Müller 'Die jüdische Entscheidung gegen Jesus nach der Apostelgeschichte' in *Les Actes des Apôtres. Traditions, rédaction, théologie* ed. J. Kremer (Leuven 1979) pp. 523-531.

10. See E. Haag 'Bund für das Volk und Licht für die Heiden (Jes. 42:6)' *Didaskalia 7* (1977) 3-18.

11. See, in addition to commentaries on Acts, M. Dibelius 'Paulus auf dem Areopag' *Aufsätze zur Apostelgeschichte* (Göttingen 1968) pp. 29-70; F. Mussner 'Anknüpfung und Kerygma in der Areopagrede (Apg. 17:22b-31)' *Präsentia Salutis* (Düsseldorf 1967) pp. 235-243.

12. See Eph. 1:23; 3:19; 4:13

13. Second Vatican Council *Dogmatic Constitution on Divine Revelation* ch. 3, art. 12.

14. See 1 Peter 1:1 f.; 2:9 f., 11.

Walter Kern

The Universality of Christianity in Hegel's Philosophy

FOR HEGEL, Christianity was the absolute religion. The main reason for this assessment, namely that Christianity is the religion of freedom, also throws light on the contemporary importance of human freedom as such. This praise of Christianity should not be regarded simply as an interesting observation, an objective statement or a chance historical discovery. It is therefore important to situate it, in a way that corresponds, at least to some extent, to Hegel's own thought, within the framework of his philosophy of the Spirit. Hegel saw Christianity as the religion of the Spirit, interpreting Spirit here as *the* reality of God and the world. The historical discussions about the relationship between Christianity and the enlightenment, the consciousness of contemporary man and world civilisation that result from this are closer to modern thinking and more worthy of our consideration than Hegel's dialectics of the Spirit, but their importance (an importance that may perhaps be exaggerated) can only be understood in the light of his dialectic of the Spirit.

1. THE HISTORICAL APPROACH:
CHRISTIANITY AS THE RELIGION OF FREEDOM

Hegel's thesis is familiar. In the East, it was believed that only '*one* is free, but because of this, freedom is merely arbitrary' and that this one was 'only a despot, not a free man, a person'. The Greeks and Romans, on the other hand, knew only 'that *some* are free', these 'some' being the citizens of the polis or the empire, 'not man as such'. It was Christianity that gave rise to the consciousness that 'man is free as man' and that 'freedom of the Spirit constitutes his particular nature'. It would, however, 'call for a long period of difficult work to incorporate this principle into man's secular being'. Hegel saw these stages as determining the great stages in the world's history and regarded the latter as 'progress in man's consciousness of freedom', which 'we have to recognise in its necessity'. The achievement of freedom was the 'ultimate purpose of the world'.[1]

Because of this, 'whole parts of the world' were unaware of the idea of freedom. Neither Plato and Aristotle on the one hand nor the Stoics on the other were conscious of it, since, for them, man was only free by virtue of a privilege of birth or philosophical wisdom. It was not until Christianity that 'the individual as such' had 'infinite value . . . by being the object and purpose of God's love and therefore destined to have its absolute relationsip with God as Spirit'. This means that 'man in himself is destined to achieve the highest freedom'.[2]

Slavery, it is true, did not cease as soon as the Christian religion was accepted, nor did freedom at once become dominant in Christian states, their governments and their constitutions. It was not, however, an undefined impulse in the Christian that was impaired by servile conditions, but 'the very substance of Christian existence', man's character as a person.[3]

The relationship with God which Christianity revealed to man released the irresistible power of change in the history of the world, the breakthrough of universal freedom. The unconditioned nature of the human person and man's dignity and fundamental freedoms—his 'human rights'—is ultimately based on its constitutive relationships with God, who alone is absolute.

2. THE SYSTEMATIC FOUNDATION:
THE DIALECTICS OF FREEDOM

Christianity is the religion of freedom because it is the religion of the Spirit. The Spirit is the total movement of God and the world that produces freedom. Freedom is an aspect and an expression of the completed reality of the Spirit. It is 'the particular being of the Spirit as its reality'[4] and the 'only purpose of the Spirit'.[5] We must attempt to explain this.

Hegel's own favourite example—and it is more than an example!—is the development of the human individual. (It should be noted that in what follows we are primarily concerned to understand Hegel's dialectics of the Spirit.) The new-born child with his completely unformed will and understanding is a *tabula rasa*. Anything can become of him. To that extent, he is simply a possibility, not a reality. He is a person only in a very general and even empty sense. He must begin to assert himself and make his way as this particular person and he does this, as a child, by reaching out with his hands and feet as well as with his senses and impulses to the world. He conquers *his* world for himself and more and more he conquers *the* world. In this process, he has to go outside himself, his vague emptiness and its vague and infinite possibilities. As a young man, he rushes towards particular goals and tries to realise them. In this attempt, he forgets himself and even loses himself. But it is only in losing himself that he finds himself. By emptying and exteriorising himself, he re-collects and interiorises himself. He expends himself on the world, but this is only apparent, since he really takes the world into himself and in this way, through the reality of the world, he himself becomes real.

This process, which is repeated with countless variations, constitutes the history of man's becoming spiritually man, the history of his individual formation. The formation of the whole of mankind and of the civilisation of the world at any period of time is recapitulated in this historical process in partial identity of greater or lesser dimensions and in complete agreement in the ideal situation that is, of course, never achieved.

What is the result of this process? The child's consciousness, which was empty, vague and general, has been filled and become characterised by the particular in its many aspects. It has extended its possibilities and enriched them by passing through the historical world, which is apparently alien and which alienates the child's and young man's consciousness from itself. It is only as a world consciousness that man's individual consciousness is consciousness of himself. By means of all the particular and definite factors, its abstractly general nature has been able to become concretely general.

At this point, it is worth noting that it is possible to distinguish certain aspects of Hegel's dialectics in the overlapping stages of the development of man's consciousness which are usually characterised (though not by Hegel himself) as the three steps of thesis, antithesis and synthesis.[6] These three aspects are, firstly, the original abstract and empty general and unmediated situation, secondly, that of negative mediation through exteriorisation into the particular and, thirdly, the general situation that has been completed and fulfilled in the concrete (from *concrescere*, to grow together) or the unmediated situation that has been mediated by the negation of the negation. Hegel also used the terms 'in itself' and 'in and for itself' for these three aspects, as well as the general, the particular and the individual. It is through these three aspects that *tollere, conservare* and *elevare*, raising up, preservation and doing away with, take place (the three concepts are contained in Hegel's one word *aufheben*) and the 'I' loses itself and in this way preserves and gains itself as a higher and complete self.

The human will[7] may try to keep its pure, boundless and undefined aspect intact. There are various ways of doing this, including suicide, political or religious fanaticism (cutting off heads), permanent revolution or total refusal. Hegel called all these forms the 'freedom of emptiness'. The will is able too to stop at the second aspect and go against its own infinite purpose by persistently pressing for individual and finite impulses to be satisfied. It will do this by choosing quite arbitrarily one thing or another. Such fortuitous and often bad choices are not, in Hegel's view, an expression of freedom. It is only if the necessity of thought is followed through and the will is directed towards the whole reality of man's world (as *the* world) that it can be 'the self-determining generality' or 'will that is free for itself—the true idea'.

Freedom, then, is not simply a quality that is present in man's will, capable of being grasped in a concept. If it were, it would be no more than the first, undefined and empty aspect. It rather constitutes the 'substance and the determination' of the will. It is the idea in the specific sense in which Hegel uses this word, that is, it is concept *and* reality or realised concept, reality that is understood and rational. In other words, freedom comes about and exists only as 'the realm of realised freedom'. This is the world of law and 'moral powers' in which men recognise each other as men. The aim of freedom is not this or that fortuitous or arbitrary choice. Freedom is, on the contrary, man's 'free will which wants free will'. It is worth noting that an echo of Hegel's idea of freedom is found in Karl Marx's view of the future society as 'an association on which the free development of each individual is the condition for the free development of all men'.[8]

3. THE SYSTEMATIC DEVELOPMENT: THE DIALECTICS OF RELIGION

In the moral world, man's will associates with itself and reflects about itself in a secular and world-wide sense. In this way, man ceases to be directed exclusively towards the finite reality and is impelled towards the free 'infinity' that is in accordance with his rational will and embraces the whole human race. Hegel did not, however, remain, in his teaching, at the stage of the self-realisation of the individual will and of (or, to express this more precisely, as) the collective human will or of the subjective and the objective spirit. His dialectics of true infinity, in which the whole of finite reality is raised up and done away with, go beyond this. This dialectical process is increasingly revealed in the phenomena of the absolute Spirit and in art, religion and philosophy. In this way, the process of freedom becomes a process of the whole of reality.

Religion presents this process to us as the history of God with the world of men. It is revealed above all as the history of the Spirit.[9]

(a) The Unity of God and Man

According to Hegel, the Christian religion is the completed and absolute religion, because it sees in Jesus and his community the reconciliation between the infinite nature of God and the finite nature of man. Isolated aspects of this reconciliation, which is accomplished in a unique and unsurpassable way in Christianity, are presented in a one-sided way in the religions of Judaism and the ancient Greek world that immediately preceded Christianity.[10] In the Jewish religion of loftiness, God is one, transcendent, infinite, omnipotent and absolute. He 'endures nothing that is related to the senses' and 'all particular aspects are extinct' in him. The secular and the finite are rejected in Yahweh. (See the first dialectical aspect.) His frightening stubbornness is glorified in the subjection of those who follow him to the law.

In the Greek religion, on the other hand, beauty is stressed and the divine appears in the harmonious brightness of the finite. The visible and tangible deities of the Greeks are, Hegel believed, nothing but the forces of nature and the powers of human civilisation personified in human forms and presented in the dimensions of human beings. Man presents himself and his needs, inclinations and passions in these gods, with the result that the divine is seen in external, particular and arbitrary categories. (See the second dialectical aspect.)

In the Christian religion, however, the general and infinite power of God is made particular and finite in the figure of the one man Jesus of Nazareth.[11] That is why it is the religion of the Spirit and the religion of truth and freedom. Hegel regarded it as essential for the Spirit to go outside itself, to be there for the other and only to come to itself in the other. God, he taught, is not God without the world. The creation of the world is his necessary manifestation of himself and the essence of God as Spirit is that he is creator.

The fact that the 'concept of religion has itself become objective', in other words, that the absolute Spirit is alive in a developed way, makes Christianity superior to all other religions. This is particularly true not only because the God of Christianity created the finite world and the human race in it, but also because he himself entered the most finite of all forms, that of a human individual, Jesus of Nazareth. Hegel tried to justify the necessity of the incarnation of God by means of speculative deduction. 'The general . . . is present only in the subjectivity of man's consciousness', he claimed, 'in the most finite of existences' or 'without mediation'. It is only in this way that 'the nature of God is revealed in the whole development of the idea'. The equality of all men is founded, according to Hegel, at the deepest level on Jesus Christ in whom the unity of the divine and the human nature and of the infinite and the finite

became a visible certainty. This results in the shortest possible conclusion: 'Slavery is insupportable!'

(b) The Crucifixion and the Presence of the Spirit[12]

The finite nature of the world and man is brought to the most extreme
point possible in Jesus' death on the cross. The necessary sin of Adam,
who is 'man in accordance with his concept', underlies the event of the
crucifixion. In other words, both man's breakthrough to his own incarnation as a civilised being and his firm orientation towards the finite evil
of his stubborn self-seeking are accomplished by his sinful knowledge of
good and evil, which makes him equal to God (Gen. 3:5, 22).

The consequence of this is death as a punishment for sin. The incarnate
God, the new and last Adam, subjected himself to death and at the same
time—as St Augustine also pointed out[13]—also overcame death. 'The
highest exteriorisation of the divine idea: "God has died; God himself is
dead" is an enormous and fearful conception', opens up 'the deepest
abyss of disunity'. But 'the death of Christ is . . . the death of that death
itself, the negation of negation', since death is, 'as the supreme way of
making finite, the raising up of and doing away with natural finiteness and
man's unmediated existence'.

The American death of God theologians, who were working for the
most part between 1960 and 1965, based their theology on Hegel, but
took short cuts and failed to see that the 'speculative Good Friday',[14]
which drew in its wake Jesus' resurrection and ascension, also included
the reconciliation of the Spirit 'as a contemplated completion'.

It was, after all, only when Jesus in the flesh had been taken out of this
world that 'the Spirit is produced' (see John 16:7), that is the Spirit of
Christ as the Holy Spirit of his community. The crucified Christ, in other
words, has 'risen' into the universal self-consciousness of his community,
of the Spirit who has become real in us as community. The visible figure of
Jesus in its external individuality of the place and period, that is, Palestine
during the reign of the Emperor Augustus, had to disappear, so that the
Spirit of Christ could reach out universally over all the zones of the world
and through all periods of human history. It was in this way that the
world-wide manifestation of God could gain its comprehensive dimensions.

The teaching of Christ—'this breaking away . . . from all that existed
previously'—was 'oriental and revolutionary' and a form of 'sans-
culotterie', the 'remedy against all servility of the Spirit'. In it, and
especially in the beatitudes of the Sermon on the Mount, Jesus proclaimed 'a complete abstraction from what is regarded as great in the
world, exaltation to the inner heaven which is open and accessible to
everyone and which makes everything else invalid'.

In the Christian community, Hegel believed that Jesus' demands became a constant and daily reality. Above all, the worship of the community proceeded from the infinite depths of the new consciousness of God and man. The eucharist he regarded as the table-fellowship of universal brotherhood in the Spirit. For Hegel, then, the community was the 'existing Spirit', the world-reality and the omni-presence of God.

(c) The History of God as the Dialectics of the Spirit[15]

Hegel's teaching about the unity of the divine and human natures in the incarnation can be applied to all the aspects of his interpretation of the Christian religion, including Christ's death on the cross, the sending of the Spirit at Pentecost and the cult of the Christian community. Taken as a whole, he believed, this 'was of importance . . . not only for the determination of human nature, but also for that of the nature of God'. What takes place here, according to Hegel, is the 'history of God' and his triune life, as that of the eternal Father, that of the Son who redeemed the created world of man and that of the Holy Spirit who completed that work.

We can try to express what this economy of the 'history of God' in and with the world means in Hegel's philosophy, not in religious categories—since the question of an immanent Trinity recedes into the background here—but in philosophical terms, those of Hegel himself. It means that the absolute goes out of its being in itself, its (eternal) universality, empties or exteriorises itself into the other of itself (creating the world and especially becoming man) and, by penetrating and including all reality (in the world-wide Church), achieves its self-conscious reality as Spirit. The history of God is the dispensation of the Spirit that necessarily permeates and receives into itself the world and the history of mankind (in accordance with the dialectical law of the Spirit). In Christianity, this dialectical dispensation of the Spirit of God, man and the world has been brought to its most radical and extreme point, where the 'most degrading death on the cross' became the foundation event. This corresponds to the boundless universal extent of the Christian mission to all nations, races and classes (see, for example, Matt. 28:19; Gal. 3:28). The universal nature of the Spirit embraces and permeates God, the world and all men. It is the basis of the universality of Christianity itself.

4. CONCRETE HISTORICAL FORMS

Hegel attempted to provide an absolute justification of Christianity as the religion of freedom in the universal dispensation of the Spirit in God and man. The nervous system of the development of modern consciousness can be found, as it were, clustered around the dialectical bone structure of his speculative plan. The result is a number of contemporary variations on the theme of the universality of Christianity.

(a) The Reformation

According to Hegel, the history of freedom was indebted to the Protestant Reformation for the decisive breakthrough that enabled its underlying Christian principle to be realised.[16] In contrast to the earlier Church, which had 'led individuals like children', the Reformed Church prompted freedom in faith and toleration. It also asserted the irreplaceable authority of the conscience as opposed to the 'slavery of authority', thus ensuring that the individual had a personal relationship with the absolute and not one that was mediated by the state, society or public morality. In addition to this, it secured the victory of the principle of subjectivity, which became the fundamental principle of the modern world. In stressing the exclusive importance of the pure gospel of Jesus Christ, Protestantism also made it possible for the respect for the freedom of others that was contained in the gospel teaching to begin to have an effect on world history.

Hegel saw the Reformation, then, as the champion of the emancipation of modern man in law, morality and freedom. For him, 'the essential content of the Reformation' was that 'man is determined by himself to be free'. The Reformation witnessed the beginning of the 'realm of the Spirit, in which God is really recognised as Spirit. The new and last banner is unfurled and the nations are gathered around it, as the flag of the free Spirit. . . . The only task that we have had and still have to do from that time until the present is to incorporate this principle into the world'.

'The Protestants achieved their revolution with the Reformation', Hegel thought, but noted that they soon returned to dogmatic and intolerant attitudes. In Europe, Christianity had to go through the experience of religious wars, in which Christians killed each other in the name of the God of love. The separation of the Christian confessions was the precondition for the freedom of man in the public life of the state and in the secular world. It was, in Hegel's own words, 'the most fortunate thing that could have happened to the Church for itself and to (philosophical) thought for its freedom and rationality'.[17]

(b) The Enlightenment[18]

Was freedom, that had been repressed once more by the Christian confessions, able to express itself in the Enlightenment? In reaction to rigid orthodoxy, what was normative at that time was not reason, but mere intellect, 'a reasoning that is opposed to rational knowledge'. According to intellect, 'the finite is not infinite, so that all mystery, that is, the speculative element in religion, is nothing to it'. Theology was there-fore also rationalistically 'reduced to a minimum of dogmas' and its content became 'extremely meagre'.

Speaking about God also became meaningless for the pietists, theologians of feeling and others who occupied the opposite theological position and who believed that only a directly experienced relationship with God was valid. Although the witness borne by my spirit to the Spirit of God called for interpretation, the most important Christian truths were explained away historically 'even by the more pious theologians'. For example, the Trinity was said to have entered Christian teaching from Greek thought, but Hegel insisted that 'the only question is whether it is true in and for itself'. Hegel in fact regarded himself as a better theologian. Because the intellectual approach of the Enlightenment (and the approach from emotion of the opponents of the Enlightenment) were so barren, the content of the Christian religion had, in Hegel's view, to be 'acquired once again conceptually; religion must seek refuge in philoso-phy'.

Hegel recognised the irrelevance of the situation in the later terror of the French Revolution 'that the chains of law and freedom are shaken off, but man's conscience is not set free and that there can be a revolution without a reformation'. Abstract, liberal words 'do not bring about this freedom of the spirit that is present in religion in true, divine freedom'. Only the whole of his rational Christian thought could, in Hegel's view, carry out the ultimate and necessary task of giving the world the sense of direction that it owed to the world, partly at least because of his own contribution to it.

(c) *Christianity and the Modern Process of Secularisation*

Modern technology and science have continued despite the Churches' opposition. It did not, however, escape Hegel's notice that biblical and Christian impulses played a part in making the empirical, scientific and secular consciousness of modern man possible.[19] Whereas the world was seen by man in ancient civilisation (and in contemporary primitive societies) as a sacral cosmos, faith in creation and the creator has taught him to regard the material world in a sober and prosaic way. 'Nature came to be divorced from God when it was distinguished from the spiritual sphere and reduced to the level of an external.' Because it is created from God out of nothing, it is the simply non-divine element without any numinous tabu. It is what Hegel himself called 'the secular earth' and man 'acquired a good conscience in its reality and in secularity'. It is both possible and permissible to study nature both in theory and in practice. 'The world must also find its reason in nature' because it is created by God. It is not inferior matter or a space inhabited by demons, but a reality that is ordered according to natural and mathematical laws, 'by measure, number and weight' (Wisd. of Sol. 11:20). It is therefore the worthy and useful object of scientific study.

On the other hand, however, Hegel recognised that the natural sciences also led to 'materialism and atheism', since 'in them, the laws of nature are treated as ultimate and as general realities'. This satisfies man intellectually, but it 'does not satisfy the living spirit or the concrete mind'. It is a legitimate form of methodical atheism for physics to ignore metaphysics, but if this is changed into a doctrinaire denial of the existence of God, science becomes mere ideology.

It is not really a question as to whether the contribution made by faith to the emergence of the distinctively modern world should be credited solely to Christianity (although there is a good case for doing this) or whether it should be assessed as being on the debit side for Christianity, especially in view of the pessimistic pronouncements and warnings of future catastrophe made in the Meadow report of 1972 (Limits to Growth). All that we can do here, on the basis of Hegel's conviction, is to point out that the only spiritual power that is capable of guiding the 'atheism of the moral world'[20] is the Christian religion of the Spirit and of freedom.

Is this the answer anticipated by Hegel to modern man's longing—from at least 1965 onwards—for ultimate values and aims that will confront the technical dream that everything can be achieved with questions about why man is here and where he is going? Hegel used the myth of the spear of the Holy Grail to illustrate the process of human knowledge as such (including the fall) and the same can perhaps be applied here to Christianity as a whole—it can heal the wound that it made.[21] Both our technological civilisation and our consciousness of basic human rights and freedoms originated in Christian Europe and Western civilisation and are now well on the way towards becoming a 'world condition'.[22] It would seem, because of this, that a secularised and anonymous universality of Christianity is also beginning to emerge in the West as a factor that is both promoting and correcting this civilisation. This prospect, however, points to certain critical objections that arise from Hegel's speculative project and his analyses of the history of modern consciousness. We must consider these in the final section that follows.

5. WILL RELIGION DO AWAY WITH ITSELF?

David Friedrich Strauss[23] believed that the individual God-man was the mythical quintessence of the *idea* of God-manhood that included in an essentially equal way all men. He resolved the tension between the extremely particular event of Jesus and the universality of the Christian

E

message and claim in favour of the second pole, with the result that, in his teaching, the historical religion of Christianity became a religious idea.

This was not in accordance with Hegel's intention. Hegel kept a firm hold on the unique and unrepeatable quality of the plain fact of the one individual and his 'most degrading death on the cross', but in such a way that he tried to deduce this fact as the extreme point to which the necessary self-emptying and exteriorisation of the Spirit of God (and the world) would go. In this way, he gave Strauss a clue for his interpretation. Just as there is only one truth, so too is there only one Spirit uniting God and man: 'The Spirit (of God) is for the spirit (of man)',[24] Hegel insisted. This is why the incarnation and Christian faith are as a whole a mystery only for the human intellect, but not for the reason of the philosopher of the Spirit.[25]

Hegelianism develops into a right or left wing according to whether it is the ideal and universal theological horizon or the particular and real anthropological elements that are extrapolated to the level of rational univocity out of *this* divine and human unity. In merging together the divine Spirit and the spirit of man in too undifferentiated a way, Hegel committed his fundamental philosophical error. Revealed religion was able, in his philosophy, to become the public religion. He was also able to say that 'there is no longer any secret in God'[26] This at least gives rise to the possible danger that religion, as a secondary phenomenon, may be absorbed into the philosophy of religion or become a mere consideration of religious ideas by philosophers of the Spirit.

This ambivalence in Hegel's speculative system can also be discerned in his analyses both of the development of man's contemporary consciousness and of the present and the future definition of the function of Christianity. (His analysis of the future of Christianity is a very reserved preview.) The relationship between religion and the secular world, as represented, in Hegel's view, by the state, is critical here. On the one hand, Hegel calls religion the source, foundation and absolute justification of life in the state. On the other hand—and here he clearly hesitates—he says 'that there is nothing that is higher or more holy than the disposition of the state or, if religion is really higher or more holy, that there is nothing in it that is either different from or opposed to the constitution of the state'.

In man's real existence, it would seem that only the secular or worldly reality counts for Hegel.[27] The state is 'the Spirit in the world' and, in the state, rational science 'extends itself like a Church to become the totality of the peculiar principle'.[28] In his later lectures on the philosophy of religion (1824 and 1827), Hegel considered the 'community of philosophy'.[29] In the meantime, he valued Protestantism very highly and did not indulge in polemics against the existing Protestant Church, because he recognised that 'the freedom of the spirit in action' and 'pacification above this reality' were to be found in the Protestant principle.[30]

The critical objections that can be raised to Hegel's philosophy of the Christian religion should not, however, make us blind to Hegel's deep conviction that the history of mankind, which was, he believed, moving towards an ultimately free human society, was the history of God himself, expressed, in a way that 'pierces the soul'[31] in the life and death on the cross of Jesus of Nazareth. We should also not underestimate the importance of his contribution to an understanding of the Jewish and Greek religions. He acquired a deep knowledge of comparative religion (most of which has, of course, now been superseded) and dealt in considerable detail with the non-Christian religions which, he believed, could only lead to Christianity as the religion of the spirit and freedom.

Translated by David Smith

Notes

1. *Die Vernunft in der Geschichte* ed. Hoffmeister (5th ed., 1955), p 62 ff.

2. *Enzyklopädie* (3rd ed.) § 482, Zusatz; cf. *Enzyklopädie*(3rd ed.) § 163, Zusatz; *Grundlinien der Philosophie des Rechts*, §§ 62, 209.

3. *Enzyklopädie* (3rd ed.) § 482 Zusatz; cf. Vernunft (Note 1), 62.

4. *Enzyklopädie* (3rd ed.) § 482 Zusatz.

5. *Vernunft* (Note 1), 64.

6. See *Einleitung in die Geschichte der Philosophie* ed. Hoffmeister (1940) pp. 100-111; *Rechtsphilosophie* (note 2), §§ 5-7; *Enzyklopädie* (3rd ed.) §§ 79-82; *Wissenschaft der Logik* ed. Lasson (2nd ed. 1934) II pp. 487-500.

7. For the following quotations, see *Rechtsphilosophie* (Note 2), §§ 5, 15, 21, 4, 1, 4, 145, 27 (cf. 21 Zusatz).

8. *Kommunistisches Manifest* ed. MEW, 4, 482.

9. For the following, in greater detail, see W. Kern 'Philosophische Pneumatologie. Zur theologischen Aktualität Hegels' *Gegenwart des Geistes*, ed. W. Kasper (Freiburg 1980) pp. 54-90; 'Menschwerdung Gottes im Spannungsfeld der Interpretationen von Hegel und Kierkegaard' *Wegmarken der Christologie* ed. A. Ziegenaus (Donauwörth 1980); 'Dialektik und Trinität in der Religionsphilosophie Hegels' *Zeitschrift für Katholische Theologie* 102 (1980) Heft 2.

10. Quotations in the following: *Vorlesungen über die Philosophie der Religion* ed. Lasson II/1 (1927) 15, 55; cf. 164, 79, 161, 142, 123.

11. Quotations in *ibid.* II/2 (1929) 34-37; I/1 (1925) 148, 200; II/2 3, 133, 138, 131.

12. Quotations in *ibid.* II/2 127, 157 f. (corrected according to the Hegel manuscript of 1821, ed. Ilting, Naples, 1978, p. 631), 167, 194, 146, 144, 145, 198.

13. *In Ioannis Evang.* 12. 10; *PL* 35. 1489: *Morte occisus mortem occidit.*

14. *Glauben und Wissen* (1802) ed. Glockner, 1, 433, according to which from the harshness of death only 'the highest totality . . . can and must rise into the brightest freedom of its form'.

15. *Religionsphilosophie* (see Note 10), II/2, 131, 54, 162.

16. See L. Oeing-Hanhoff 'Hegels Deutung der Reformation' *Hegel* (Lille 1970) pp. 239-257. Quotations from *Vorlesungen über die Philosophie der Weltgeschichte* ed. Lasson (2nd edn. 1923), 827, 873, 882, 881, 925.

17. *Rechtsphilosophie* (see Note 2) § 270 = ed. Glockner 7, 362.

18. Quotations in *Weltgeschichte* (see Note 16) 916; *Religions-philosophie* (Note 10) I/1, 36, 42, 46; II/2, 231; *Weltgeschichte* 932, 931.

19. See W. Kern 'Atheismus—Christentum—Emanzipierte Gesellschaft. Zu ihrem Bezug in der Sicht Hegels' *Zeitschrift für Katholische Theologie* 91 (1969), pp. 289-321; Quotations in *Weltgeschichte* 454 (cf. 458), 747, 876 (cf. 868), 912, 916.

20. *Rechtsphilosophie* (see Note 2) *Vorrede* = ed. Glockner 7, 25.

21. *Religionsphilosophie* (see Note 10) II/2, 105 (cf. 110, 124).

22. *Vorlesungen über die Geschichte der Philosophie* ed. Glockner 19, 511; *Religionsphilosophie* II/2, 150.

23. *Das Leben Jesu kritisch betrachtet* (Tübingen 1836) II pp. 732-744; see also W. Kern 'Eine Wirklinie Hegels in deutscher Theologie; Christusereignis und Gesamtmenschheit' *Zeitschrift für Katholische Theologie* 93 (1971) 1-28.

24. *Religionsphilosophie* I/1 51 and frequently repeated *passim*.

25. *Ibid.* II/2 77 f.

26. *Ibid.* I/1 75.

27. *Weltgeschichte* 928, 920; cf. 917, 923.

28. *Rechtsphilosophie,* § 270 = ed. Glockner, 7, 349, 357.

29. *Religionsphilosophie* II/2, 232.

30. *Weltgeschichte* 920, 923 (cf. 925).

31. *Religionsphilosophie* II/2, 152 (cf. 144).

Christian Duquoc

Christianity and its Claim to Universality

CHRISTIANITY is seen by its adherents as having a universal mission: it is not a religion for a people or an ethnic group, but a call to all mankind. This conviction has been expressed in various ways, of which the most specific has been, 'Outside the Church there is no salvation'. For the ordinary believer this axiom meant that there was no hope of sharing in the eternal Kingdom without effectively belonging to the historic community of followers of Christ: the Church.

Inspired by this conviction, the Christian West set out on a remarkable course of missionary expansion. The evidence we possess of vocations to proclaim the gospel in distant lands, particularly in the nineteenth century, testifies to the spread of the belief that there is no hope of salvation outside the Church. This explains excesses of zeal such as the forcible baptism of dying children: how could the violence done to parental feeling or local custom be compared to the eternal happiness thereby bestowed on the child?

Of course, one can point out that the better-informed theologians never understood the axiom in such a literal manner. But this is not the point: the widespread conviction is a better index of how Christians saw the universality of their faith and how this affected Western societies in their relationships with other cultures than the elaborations of theologians.

The way in which the universality of the faith was generally presented acted as a spur to intolerance toward societies living by other beliefs. Christianity's general claim to universality and conviction of its obvious rights have often produced socially destructive results. Universality, once it is represented by a group and becomes its property, is never a simple notion or just a theoretical concept; it becomes operational by virtue of its incarnation in the group. The axiom 'No salvation outside the Church' becomes a sanction for the social exclusion of those who are not members of the group of the 'saved': they are regarded as already belonging to the city of the evil one and treated as such.

So the question of universality is not a subject for abstract debate, but concrete, i.e., historical. It would be dishonest to examine intentions alone; we need to investigate the way a group puts the values it holds into social practice and to evaluate the effects produced by its convictions. It is not enough to say that 'all men are saved in Jesus Christ'; we need to examine the visible consequences of this belief at work in history. So my starting-point is not this affirmation, but the challenges presented by the errors and blunders committed by a Church convinced of its right to represent the whole of humanity and to act for its future happiness—'by their fruits you shall know them'.

My considerations on this subject unfold as follows: first, an examination of the problems resulting from the behaviour of a Church convinced of its universality; second, a study of the question of the universality of Christ; and finally, an analysis of the ethical and political consequences of this for the Church.

1. THE HISTORICAL CHURCH AND UNIVERSALITY

'I have loved Jacob and hated Esau' (Mal. 1:2-3, quoted by Paul in Rom. 9:13). The Church, in its historical embodiment, is hardly separable from the effects induced by the feeling of being chosen. Being chosen is first and foremost differentiating oneself from others through a privilege they do not have the honour of sharing in. Its end result is to exclude the others from the world in which the choice brings the chosen to live. We are not here dealing with some minor privilege, but with the possibility of sharing in absolute happiness, from which the non-chosen are thereby, hypothetically, excluded. So the non-chosen becomes the outcast.

I am not claiming that these were dogmatic affirmations, but I do maintain that the doctrine of election has had social effects not necessarily according with dogmatic statements. A medieval chronicle I read stated that crusaders were convinced of despatching the Muslims they killed to hell.

It might seem paradoxical to saddle the Church with a general consensus and manner of behaving that seem more appropriate to the synagogue, a consensus and behaviour the Church broke with when it affirmed that in Jesus Christ salvation had been brought to the very pagans. The fact is that once the Church stopped being a minority group devoid of power and, after the conversion of Constantine, acquired influence in affairs of State, it ceased, with a few rare exceptions, to practise toward pagans the tolerance it had previously sought for itself.

A superficial judgment would see this contradiction as simply an application of the maxim that power corrupts. I would admit that this is an element, but would not see it as the root cause, which I see in a double conviction: Divine providence has granted Christianity the victory as proof of its universal truth, and it behoves the convinced Christian to impose this truth on men—for their own good—through the law, which does not exclude the use of violence.

The first conviction stems from a readily comprehensible enthusiasm: a group which had been persecuted for centuries and yet was convinced of being God's chosen people and of representing the future of humanity, suddenly, and apparently miraculously, finds itself in power; this it sees as the fulfilment of promises and even as a divine sign of the forthcoming advent of the Kingdom, or at least as an invitation to anticipate the Kingdom here and now through an ethical and political system based on the gospel, with the Church as its privileged agent of execution. This conviction found the element needed for the actual realisation of its universality in the notion that truth alone has a right to social expression—and that the visible Church is the best guarantor of this truth. The Church thereby inclines toward legitimising its universality by means deriving from its political power.

The second conviction, the need to impose universal truth by means of the law, finds its justification in the theological axiom 'Outside the Church there is no salvation'. In theological terms this axiom means that recognition of Christ as Saviour is inseparable from insertion in the community that witnesses to him. It does not specify what this insertion consists of.

Though this axiom can be given a tolerant interpretation theologically, its sociological effects were far less benign: it had the effect of denying those outside the ranks of the visible Church—Jews, pagans, Muslims—the civic rights accorded to Christians. So Christianity became the operative force behind the legal and social establishment of the Church's pre-eminence and claim to declare, in theory and in practice, what men had to do to reach their goal. Those who, from choice or heredity, disagreed in practice, were granted the right to a civic existence on sufferance alone.

This widespread ecclesial political stance had a serious implication: Must the theological proposition on the universal role of the Church lead to social intolerance? If so, the ideology of Christian universality would be favouring a system of power politics which confirmed its legitimacy by dominating all ethnic and cultural forms which could not be assimilated to the Church. In this case, one has to ask whether the movement founded by Jesus Christ can justify the social working of this universality. But before examining the nature of the universality promised by Jesus, I think we should enquire into the source of the questions: a less abstract view of 'the universal' for a start, and then the experience of the dispersal of the divine. These points need clarification before referring to the universal nature of Jesus.

Seeing universality as something less abstract means seeing it not as a norm, a positive prescription applicable to each and every situation. Take a simple example: the norm governing marriage in Catholicism. We know the formula: monogamy and indissolubility. We are here dealing with a norm, since it implies a positive imposition of a form of social relationship and a rule governing the use of sexuality, on principle excluding other forms as unworthy of the Kingdom. This norm is universal since, at least hypothetically, it allows of no exception and excludes all variants. Form is identified with absolute. Outside this norm, no sexual relations are worthy of man and woman. As a result, since this Western form of marriage is the only human one, it must be spread to all cultures. The only way of escaping this conclusion is to see the Catholic norm for marriage as having universal value not as a prescription for a social structure, but as an ideal against which to judge all relationships between men and women. I call the identification of universality and norm or specific rule abstract because it excludes all other possible forms, by stigmatising them as immoral. But such abstraction has specific consequences.

The necessary distinction between the norm and the universal would seem to be applicable to the Catholic Church. In the course of its history, the Roman Catholic Church has adopted various forms of government, organisation and thought as a—doubtless necessary—reaction to specific challenges or evolutionary needs. But the Catholic Church, with its consciousness of being the witness to him who is the Way, the Truth and the Life, tends to picture its structure, government and organisation as an imperative norm and a prescriptive instrument of salvation, in that they derive from the commands of its founder. From then on, its practical universality becomes identified with its visible organisation as the obligatory mediation for the encounter with Jesus Christ and God. Applied to missionary expansion, this means that local customs and traditions will have to yield to an imported norm. An example of how imperative this norm can become is that of ordained ministers, where the needs of communities with no Western history are not taken into account. And an example of how fixed it can become historically is provided in Western society itself, where the new place of woman in society counts for nothing.

If the universality of the Church is a norm, it engenders destruction of other modes of being and imposes its own organisation, thought, hierarchical structure as earthly reflections of a divine, and therefore immutable, order. Outside this norm, there can be no experience of universality, unless seen as a contradiction or at best a preparation. This gives rise to practical obstacles to the spread of the gospel, since necessary conditions for conversion become more burdensome than conversion itself, involving renunciation of one's own history and culture. So it would be better to regard the universality of the Church as subject to the same conditions as universality in any society: bound by forms and laws that must always be relative, since no society is the ideal incarnate.

This relativity is confirmed by consideration of the second element: the dispersal of the divine.

Many Christians have sincerely believed that adoration of a god or gods in other religions is a form of idolatry. Believing themselves to be the only ones to worship the true God, Christians have felt obliged to impose adoration of him on everyone else. We know what effects this produced on the Indians of America. These near-fanatical convictions are now weakening as we come to a better understanding of other religions, and many Christians appreciate that a high degree of spirituality, true detachment, real love of one's neighbour and an admirable mystic sense can be found in other religious traditions, and that the Catholic Church does not have a monopoly of the divine. It is only a short step from there to thinking, as some hasty spirits do, that all religions are but variations of the same religious sense. So, after having defended the almost fanatical view of our originality as Christians for so long, we seem to be ready to abandon our claims to any particular universality.

Fear of this happening is salutary: it shows the danger of quick dismissal of any relationship to God outside the Church as valueless. Admitting the value of a relationship to God outside the Church means questioning the nature of the universality of our link with God and the validity of the concepts we use to express it. Naturally, the dispersal of the divine in other religions sets the limits of our universality—personally, I am inclined to think that this dispersal guides us toward a way of conceiving the universal that shows more respect to others and makes us more attentive to our own situation as a Church. And definitely keeps us more faithful to the inspiration of the New Testament.

Those who absolutise the Church will see much to fear in this new outlook. Its consequences, however, fit the facts of ecclesial history much better. It has too long been thought that provided one loved God and practised virtue, the government of things and of men would turn out for the best. In point of fact, a number of holy men, heroic in virtue, such as certain inquisitors, have, objectively, been criminals working with selfless dedication to make the world a less habitable place. They had no doubt of the universal as the ecclesial form designed for the good of all mankind.

Since then, we have become wary of the power of the best principles embodied in policies or Churches to make men happy or our world tolerable. The Churches themselves have become more modest about their power to influence the course of events, seeing what troubles have been caused, within their own bodies, by application of the highest ideals. Universality thus ceases to be valid or worthy of study outside a specific, contingent application. Universality is seen in the capacity a law has to change, a society to reform, a hierarchy to stand down; not in its strength of imposition and prescription, but in its ability to question and accommodate. The Kingdom of God is beyond our imagination, but what can be done in a particular situation to make the world a better place is not. Beyond the particular achievement, the *ad hoc* decision, the ever-changing situation, there is no universal. The artist who paints a particular picture might regret all the possible pictures excluded by the one he has just finished, might think the universal is the sum total of all possibilities. But in fact these possibilities are only linked to the universal by the particular work that enables one to evoke other ideas. The universal takes shape in the particularity of one work to the extent that this work leaves others the power to come about. It is precisely its limitation as offering another work the chance to develop that marks its universality. But, one might object, this leads the Church—which claims to embody God's action in history and contemplate the perfect icon of God in Christ—into contradiction: does its historic bent to exclusivity not stem from its consciousness of offering the perfect setting for our relationship with God, thereby abolishing all space other than its own, unlike the work of art which opens up others? The answer to this objection is, I think, to be found not in the Church, but in him to whom it is a witness: Jesus Christ.

2. THE UNIVERSALITY OF JESUS CHRIST

Having started with the axiom, 'Outside the Church there is no salvation' and seen that, however true it might be in theory, its social effects have often been destructive, we now need to abandon it and replace it with a Christological principle: 'Only in the name of Jesus can we find salvation'. Personally, I consider the universality of this principle to belong to a different order to the ecclesiological axiom, by virtue of him to whom it testifies.

Confessing the universality of historical Christianity ultimately means defending the claim of one group to speak and act for the benefit of the whole of humanity to and in the name of him who is deemed to legitimise the claim. In other words, we have to see whether the intolerant manner in which the Church conceived and embodied this claim can be justified by him to whom the Church is witness.

The answer is not simple, and in the space of an article must necessarily be schematic. For the sake of clarity, I would like to distinguish three modes of legitimisation: the pertinence of the message, the prophetic quality of the messenger, and the absence of the risen Christ.

(a) The pertinence of the message

Contemporary exegesis sees the transition from Christ's preaching of the Kingdom to the Church's proclamation of Christ as a major problem. Here, we must leave the exegetical aspect of the question aside and concentrate of the theological implications of this switch.

The figure of Christ tends to be substituted for the message to the extent that it is, for practical purposes, substituted for that of God. The consequences of this substitution seem to me to fall into two categories: on one hand the figure of the witness adoring Christ is favoured at the expense of the individual figure of Jesus; on the other, what is today called the subversive aspect of the message is forgotten.

First the witness is favoured, and this in practice means the Church, in its adoration of Christ and its celebration of his worship. The result of this practice is the identification of Christ with God, omitting to make clear that it was Jesus of Nazareth who was proclaimed the Christ. If 'Christ' is, in its meaning of Messiah of Israel taken as Messiah of the whole human race, henceforth the name universally given to Jesus the Nazarene, then the universality of Christ is based on, governed by and shaped by the originality of the figure of Jesus, in his true individuality: a Galilean Jew, put to death for subversion by the governor Pontius Pilate, the representative of the Roman occupying power.

If one respects the overall tenor of the New Testament, it is, I believe, impossible to separate the universal figure of Christ—the justification for his witness, the Church, to be a universal group—from the individual figure of Jesus. This is what gives weight to, and limits, the figure substituted for God, Christ. It is Jesus, in fact, who prevents us from substituting Christ for God, by maintaining the necessary separation between Christ and God, and between Christ and his historical witness, the Church: a separation or distancing which imposes a particular form and operation of the universal.

This necessary return to the figure of the Nazarene is made through the memory of his message. The gospels are not biographies; they are the active memory of prophetic words and deeds. To forget the message for the sake of exaltation of the personage leads finally to exalting the witness, since the distance established by the pertinence of the message to the witnessing group is abolished. Hiding the message behind the messenger in this way has one particular result: the message is universalised by the exaltation of the messenger at Easter. The purpose of Easter can and should be conceived in a different way: it is inseparable from Good

Friday, which represents the sanctioning of the message. It is because the message has a universal destination that it is exalted in its messenger at Easter. It is not sufficient to proclaim Jesus as Lord of all to be his witness; first the message must be put into practice. The message removes all possibility of identifying the Church with the Kingdom, the Church with Christ. Scripture, as the means by which the preaching of Jesus is brought to our knowledge, says once and for all that the Church is something particular and that it is not the Kingdom, that its laws cannot be other than the laws of this preaching, of which no-one can claim ownership, since it calls all men, including Christians, into question. In this sense, the message is pertinent, determining the prophetic quality of the messenger.

(b) The prophetic quality of the messenger

The universality of Jesus is based in the first analysis on the pertinence of his message; this means the personage is secondary to the message. This has too often been forgotten in Christological thinking. The message alone, which does not favour the power ideology of any group, chosen— as in the gospel situation—or not, is capable of establishing an effective and efficacious distance between the social and often immediate interests of the group and the evangelical movement immanent in the message of Jesus. If the Christian group has henceforth some claim to universality, it is by virtue of the message it proclaims. Ernst Bloch has effectively highlighted this power of the message by opposing the Bible to the politics of Churches.

Hiding the message behind the personality of the messenger tends to deprive the messenger of his prophetic quality: it provides a transcendant justification for the wishes of a people or a class. The prophetic quality of Jesus is seen in the fact that his message cannot be identified with any ideology designed to ensure the survival of a group. Seen in this light, the basic difference between Catholicism and Protestantism takes on con- siderable importance: at the risk of over-simplifying, I would say the Protestant sensibility restores autonomy and prophetic power to the message, disengaging it on principle from the legitimising ownership of a group; Catholic sensibility, on the other hand, tends to appropriate the message, and sometimes, through the devices of tradition and the magis- terium, to deform its autonomy. Of course, the underlying intentions of both groups are to safeguard the freedom of the message. History proves that neither form of approach to the message is perfect, with the Pro- testant confessions permissively allowing interpretation to be chained to the fashion of an age, with the result that the gospel becomes a religious accompaniment to a particular culture, and the Catholic Church chaining interpretation of Scripture to its own chains. It may be that the present division of the Churches is the best way of ensuring the autonomy of the message and witnessing to the prophetic quality of its author; this division frees the message from the interests of particular groups, marks out the distance between the Churches and the Kingdom, encourages a universality of interrogation and not of prescription.

The prophetic quality of Jesus comes to us through his message. To understand it fully, we need to see how Jesus' behaviour with regard to the then dominant state religion, behaviour of which many of his parables are an interpretation, fits into the overall message. Here, though, there is space only to stress that exaltation of the messenger loses its depth and ultimately its prophetic quality if it is not structured by proclamation of the gospel, proclamation that never ceases to call the Church to conversion. The absence of the prophetic leader underlines this view still further.

(c) *The absence of the risen Christ*

The autonomy of the message in relation to the social interests of the Church is confirmed by the absence of the Christ, to whom the Church is witness.

The message represents the preaching of Jesus. God accredits this prophet by resurrecting him, thereby also ensuring the universality of his message, though this is derived from itself and not from the act of Resurrection. The event that ensures the universality of the message is the means by which the messenger absents himself. What the disciples sought from the message, as evidenced by their request at the moment of the ascension, was to confer the leadership of the Kingdom on the person they saw as having escaped from historical contingency and mortal destiny: they besought Jesus, as Christ, to transform the conditions of our earthly existence. Just when this hope seemed about to be fulfilled—the victim of Good Friday having become the Lord for ever—what they least expected happened: the leader removed himself. He left the Good News to witnesses, whose sole justification they had to find in the pertinence of the message. The absence of the leader confirms the absence of any impositon or prescription. Jesus, in his capacity as Christ, did not order the leaders of communities to organise the Kingdom on his behalf, but to be witnesses to the Good News. They were not to be substitutes for a leader. The absence of the leader signifies the pre-eminence of the message over its personal embodiment. The putting of the message into practice by the witness group will verify not the pertinence of the message, but the prophetic authenticity of the group.

If these principles seem to hold good, if the pertinence of the message, the prophetic quality of the messenger and his absence qualify the universality claimed by the Church, then certain ethical and political requirements affecting the Church must follow from this.

3. ETHICAL AND POLITICAL REQUIREMENTS AFFECTING THE CHURCH

The way of approaching the universality of the Church proposed here seems to me to bring two requirements in the field of ethics and two obligations in the field of politics. In ethics, the two requirements can be summed up as tolerance and conversion. In politics, they can be described as respect for the autonomy of civil societies and militancy on behalf of groups lacking in authority and often in hope.

The double ethics requirement—tolerance and conversion—also affects the inner life of the Church as well as its relation with civil societies and other religions.

Tolerance first: the word has been over-used, and is often confused with permissiveness, being taken in this sense to designate a state of detachment from the basic problems of individual and social life. True tolerance does from spring from *taedium vitae,* but is strength. Those who believe in the truth of Christ renounce all imposition of this truth through sanctions, within the Church as well as without. They hope the truth of Christ bears its own power of conversion within itself and would rather not see it in action than employ means that obscure its dynamism. The Cross is integral to this tolerance. Jesus used his prophetic freedom and his word was often a sword, but he never prescribed his word. So the Church should witness to the universality of its vocation by preferring the often painful choice of freedom to the easy imposition of its views through sanctions. This does not imply renouncing the regulation of its faith, but setting about it in a different manner. Tolerance can be understood as the Church withdrawing or effacing itself in relation to what it testifies to, placing more confidence in the Spirit than in its power as a group. This self-effacement is the condition for the appearance of an interrogatory universality.

Then conversion: this word no longer possesses its New Testament force. In its original sense it means a coming round in the spirit, and it is in this sense a permanent requirement, since the Church is not the Kingdom. The message of Jesus is that the law of survival of the group should not become the law of the Church. Let us just imagine the Church taking seriously, as a group, the words of Jesus in Matt. 5:23: 'If, when you are bringing your gift to the altar, you suddenly remember that your brother has a grievance against you, leave your gift where it is before the altar. First go and make peace with your brother . . .' Worship can only have universal meaning when it can efface itself before the need for reconciliation.

Or imagine taking that other saying of Jesus seriously: 'Do not call any man on earth "father"; for you have one Father, and he is in heaven' (Matt. 23:9). This would imply that hierarchy, so rooted in the Catholic

Church, could only be justified by practising self-effacement in order to let the only God shine through.

If the real worshippers of God are those who worship in spirit and in truth, as Jesus said to the Samaritan woman (John 4:23), then the outward forms of worship practised by the Church must take a lower place. So universality is written in the margins as the hope of a liberty not yet come to pass. Also, as soon as the Church puts its structure, organisation, and even orthodoxy in the forefront of its preoccupations, it betrays the movement to conversion stemming from the gospels, ceases to be an interrogation for all mankind and quite soon comes to think of itself as the universal society that must be universally imposed.

The political requirements complete the ethical ones: respect for the autonomy of civil societies, militancy on behalf of groups without authority and without hope.

Tolerance, an act of faith in the power of the truth of Christ, has a political aspect: respect for the autonomy of societies. This respect is applicable to all human creations, including ethical systems. It is normal for the Church to make its views known; it would be abnormal for it to apply pressure to make its opinions accepted. The political relationship is also an act of conversion on its part, since it is in its retreat from its power to dominate, even for good, that the Church bears witness to its universal calling.

Respect does not imply indifference toward the misfortunes and injustices to which civil society is prone. Tolerance is not naivety. Weakness and non-violence are not complicity. There are men without hope, those who will never know the freedom to eat, to educate themselves; whose labour will only go to enrich others. The Church must become their voice, as Jesus became the voice of the outcasts of his time. The Church must also become their companion and sometimes even their home, the refuge of their fragile freedom. In this way it will proclaim to the world that although the Kingdom has not yet come, it can be glimpsed in the margins of history, since men and women without hope or dignity are learning that a man, Jesus, is near and that the world will never deserve the name of 'new' as long as their cries are heard.

Universality is not an abstraction; it is concrete, but not the sort of concrete out of which the utopic realisation of the Absolute can be built in the Church. Universality happens on the fringes, an incandescence burning away all idolatries, particularly those of Churches which, in the name of Jesus, have sometimes added to the sum total of unhappiness in the world—through failing to distance themselves from the Kingdom which for ever imposes the message to which they are the witnesses here below.

Translated by Paul Burns

Joseph Comblin

The Current Debate on Christian Universality

WHAT ONE would like to be able to do in this article is to detail the transition from an ecclesiastical, abstract concept of universalism to a concrete universalism pertaining to the poor. Unfortunately, if we put ourselves in the position of the peripheral Churches, or, in particular, of Latin America, we are forced to recognise that the die has not yet been cast: we are in open conflict.

On one hand, we have a Church whose origins are among the poor. Yet we also have, on the other hand, a league of political and religious forces determined to stand in the way of any form of liberating Christianity and to revive the concept of 'traditional' Christianity, dedicated to its 'spiritual' tasks. In this league, precedence is accorded to strongly 'Christian' authoritarian governments who maintain that they are building or restoring a fixed, conservative, verticalist society founded on 'Christianity'. Supporting these governments they are also the traditional aristocratic classes and the new *elites*, who view the ecclesiastical, abstract concept of universalism as the basis of society. As a result, the nation's entire resources go to ensure the survival or the reconstitution of this universalism.

It is hardly surprising to see governments and social *elites* give their full support not only to decadent integrist movements, but especially to expanding apocalyptic sects. Large landowners with 'strong Catholic' views favour the arrival of sects like the Mormons on their lands, because they know that these sects will make their peasants forget their earthly lot to concentrate exclusively on thoughts of heaven and hell. These sects are growing fast; they have considerable resources at their disposal, and receive ample political and social support. This is why we say that the outcome of the debate is still undecided.

In Latin America, the debate about true universality is not an academic one: thousands have died as a result of abandoning their traditional abstract universalism and discovering a new Christian concept of universalism, that of the liberation of the poor.

For the Church, the debate about the true meaning of universality is not new either; it has always been central to the debate on the meaning of mission. The new element is the moment of history in which we live.

Up to the present day, Christianity has been in a constant state of growth, and this growth has accompanied the conquest of the world by Western society. Missionaries have always disagreed on the reason for this growth: whether it was due to the conquest of the world by the West or, in spite of this conquest, to the compensating action of missionaries who were, on a personal level, independent of the conquerors. Both these missionaries who had links with conquering powers and those who were opposed to them gave the credit for the victory of Christianity to themselves. In victory, everyone gives himself the credit for what happened; but then, everyone is content, and these issues are not serious.

The issue becomes serious when victory ceases, when the growth of Christianity seems to have come to a halt. Then, everyone blames 'the others'. According to some, the Church is in a state of recession because she has ceased to rely on those powers which have always come to her aid, and because she is losing her way in the maze of political options which are outside her jurisdiction. According to others, the Church has been halted because she is tied to historical factors which have no future.

1. APOCALYPTIC UNIVERSALITY

Now, as always, the most fundamental debate deals with eschatology: Does history have meaning for Christianity or not?

Apocalyptism predates Christ; it had a profound effect on Judaism during the final centuries of its pre-Christian history. It had an effect on important sectors of the primitive Church. Up to the end of the seventeenth century it was an important constituent of official Christianity. It had a profound influence on the missionary movement. For centuries, innumerable Christians, and especially those among them who were the most 'aggressively' Christian, spent their lives waiting for the Last Judgement. They lived as though the end of the world was immediate, as though the world had lost its significance in the face of imminent eternity. Even today, the most virulent, fast-growing form of Christianity is that of the sects which proclaim the impending last judgement.

For apocalyptic Christianity, history and all its distinctions are meaningless. Domination or liberation, wealth or poverty, dictatorship, slavery, war or peace, all this is of no importance, of no account; all this is

F

overshadowed by the only important consideration: we have a soul which is urgently in need of salvation. There is no time to think of anything else. When the gates of heaven are open before him, is there any man who will then ask himself whether he is lord or slave, rich or poor, free citizen or king's subject?

In the apocalyptic scheme of things, there is one single reality, the same for all. Real universality is the universality of the last judgement, of heaven and hell, the universality of the soul subjected to that judgement. Apocalyptic Christianity is universal, because it sees all men reduced to their common factor: the problem of saving their soul. Nothing else is important.

'Saving one's soul' is a universal process, the same everywhere: it entails having recourse to the 'means of salvation'. The first of these is baptism. Then comes the other sacraments, the utterances of faith, the acts of belonging to the Church, and all the secondary means she proposes (blessing in articulo mortis, indulgences, etc.). The task of the Church and of missionaries is 'to save souls', as many souls as possible. To achieve this end, it is necessary to draw on every resource.

Faced with the urgent task of saving souls, the circumstances of salvation become insignificant. It would be readily acknowledged that the conversion of the American Indians and of the slaves imported from Africa was carried out in deplorable conditions. But, in the final analysis, the fact that the indigenous population and the Africans were reduced to a condition of slavery is of little importance in the light of the immense benefit accorded them by the salvation of their souls. Missionaries will close their eyes to contingencies, seeing only the essential, the salvation of souls. What counts is the salvation of the greatest number, even if providence, in pursuit of this aim, makes use of the most incomprehensible circumstances. The gravest mis-deeds of the conquerors have had this favourable effect: millions saved their souls, which they would have lost had they not been conquered, exiled, deported or reduced to slavery.

Saint Thomas himself thought that the worst tortures endured by heretics were nothing when compared with the salvation of their souls resulting from the final repentance that could be induced by these tortures. Therefore, the missionaries thought a fortiori that the sufferings of the Indians and the black slaves were of little importance when compared with the benefits of eternal salvation.

Similarly, many Christians today think the Church must consider the fact that, owing to the present existence of dictatorships in Latin America, many more souls can be saved, the sacraments can be administered without difficulty and more people avail themselves of the means of salvation: God knows how to use even bad means to serve a good end, the saving of souls. This is why a large sector of the Church, the most powerful from an economic and social point of view, serves as a support for the strongly 'Christian' dictatorships of 'National Security'. That does not prevent these Christians from condemning individual instances of abuse or from regretting the existence of practices incompatible with the tenets of social Christianity; but such errors can in no way be measured against the incomparable benefit of allowing souls to be saved.

In the same way, those sects which are in the process of conquering Latin America readily led their services to large multinational enterprises eager to canvass or to gather information, who pay generously for such services: one may use the Devil's money to rescue souls from him, should he be foolish enough to think that he will have the last word.

The 'thirst for souls' has had a considerable part to play in the growth of missionary activity. It must be acknowledged that the apocalyptic scheme is endowed with an extraordinary dynamism. Not only does it adapt itself to conquest, but it is, itself, a conqueror. The apocalyptic mentality leads naturally to a move to conquer souls on a universal scale. It is not deterred by anything, for the importance of the end result totally detracts from incidental historical circumstances.

That is why the apocalyptic scheme has a future ahead of it. There is always the danger that a Church, anxious about the darkness of the future, will resort to this solution which is so easy, so effective, and has such deep roots in history!

2. THE UNIVERSALITY OF CHRISTENDOM

The majority of those critical of Christendom trace it back to Constantinism. That is a mistake. Christendom predates Constantine with regard to the essential nature of its mentality and of its objectives. Christendom existed in Israel itself. It did not originate in the Church as a result of the political or cultural forces of the Roman Empire. There would have been one or more forms of Christendom even without any suggestion of a Roman Empire. The Church carried Christendom with her from the beginning as a part of her Jewish heritage. The Roman Empire was able to give a distinctive historical flavour to Christendom: it did not create it. The Empire was able to use Christendom, but not to set it up. Christendom preceded it.

The essentials of Christendom were contained in the Judaism of the Scribes and the Pharisees, according to the description given in the New Testament. It consists of two basic elements.

In the first place is the conviction that *we* are the kingdom of God: we are the universal reality of the kingdom of God; everything which is outside us is also outside the kingdom of God. Our universality may seem very small; that does not matter. Did not Jesus say: 'Do not fear, little flock'? If we are few in number, that illustrates the parable of the mustard seed; that is to say, the universality of our being must remain hidden because of the laws of the kingdom of God.

Just as the Pharisees see themselves as heirs to the prophets and to the Israel of the Exodus, so Christendom sees itself as heir to the first Christians, to the martyrs, to the Fathers of the Church. When we go into the Catacombs of Rome, we, as Catholics, feel proud because we see ourselves as the descendants of the martyrs and not of those responsible for their martyrdom. When we read the Acts of the Apostles, we are proud of Barnabas, and we do not recognise ourselves in the figures of Ananias and Sapphira (despite the very striking resemblance to the contemporary west). Christendom is a Church which forgets its historicity in order to identify itself with the ideal model of the primitive Church.

In Christendom, we are the poor of God. If we are rich, we should thank God for it. In reality, we were poor. But God has fulfilled his beatitudes: he has given the earth to the poor. Praise God! We are the small and the humble: if we are powerful, it is because God has exalted the humble. We are the foolish; if we have become wise, it is because God has given wisdom to the foolish. The Americans still see themselves playing the part of the poor Puritans of the Mayflower, or, alternatively, of those wretched Irishmen forced by famine to flee their country. Thus, as Christians, we see ourselves playing the part of the first disciples, not that of the rich young man who could not give up his possessions, but that of Peter and the apostles. So we are, as it were, in name or by profession, the heirs of the saints and the martyrs. Just like the Pharisees who venerated the tombs of the prophets and did not realise that they killed them.

To that is added the second element of Christendom: the acceptance of all that the past has added as coming from God. For the Pharisees, all the traditions accumulated by them or by their ancestors were as precious as the Word of God: these traditions had so entered into the Word of God that they could no longer be separated from it. In the same way, in Christendom, all that history has added to the primitive Church is irreversible. The entire historical development of Christianity is as vital a part of this Christianity as its origins. All the acquisitions of history are valid and must be accepted. To become a Christian is to accept fully the heritage of history: this heritage is a part of Christian universality.

Until fairly recently, ecclesiology regarded the history of the Church as a homogenous development. All that had been preserved from the past remained by virtue of divine will. God made history sacred. Whatever had triumphed in the Church was destined to triumph and retained the seal of sanctity.

In these conditions, the fact that one aspect of this historical Christianity originated under the influence of Constantinism or of Hellenistic philosophy is of little importance. The origin here is not important; what is important is that these things came into the Church. Once in, they could no longer leave — whether formulations of dogma, liturgy, the structure of the clergy, or the pattern for the diocese.

In Christendom, the aim of missionary work is to make 'Christians', that is to say, people who accept all this heritage. If certain groups of people refuse to be converted on these terms, that is a shame, but the fault is theirs. Missionary work can only be conceived as an extension of past history. If God has allowed historical forces to give to Christendom the historical weight that it carries, then he will not abandon his work. Missionary activity must maintain its original impetus.

As the Church today and the historical forces which underlie it are considered to constitute Christian universality, pastoral work is reduced to a sort of geopolitics. The destiny of Christianity is linked to that of the West. It is necessary to gamble on the universality of the West and, as in the past, profit from the capacity for growth in the West. This is the course followed implicitly by all the established churches, despite explicit declarations to the contrary which are the sheerest opportunism. We are relying on the solidity of the past and on the universality of the West, and this allows us to go on without making any fundamental change, as the whole of the past remains both valid and effective.

Neither apocalyptic universality, nor the universality of Christendom necessarily includes a pattern of conquest or domination. Nevertheless, they both adjust to it very easily. They do not hesitate to place themselves in the path of any conquest: they find many advantages in this and are able to offer any necessary justifications for it. They explain that, after all, very little objection was ever made in the past in connection with evangelical conquest.

Elsewhere, the specific circumstances surrounding the development of Christendom in the west, as in the east, in the area of growth particular to the Roman Empire and to its heirs, gave missionary activity itself a certain element of conquest: universality became domineering, owing to its involvement in the Graeco-Roman world.

3. GRAECO-ROMAN UNIVERSALITY

The close union between the Christian Church and the Graeco-Roman world (and the European civilisation which continues it) has given added emphasis to several of the characteristics of Christendom.

In the first place, Christianity feels itself to be universal inasmuch as it is an established, structured and stable entity; it is universal because it is the universe ready-organised, the cosmos ready-ordered. Secondly, it is an historical whole and feels it is capable of integrating any people or society that may materialise. Thus it is that the discovery of America was not an impossible challenge: from their first meeting with the unknown people of America, the Europeans knew for sure that they would be able to integrate them. They knew that they could make them into good Christians and good, obedient subjects, members of an established Christendom. Universality does not have to be worked at; it has been achieved. All that remains is for it to integrate whatever may yet be discovered. Should this latter refuse integration, that is no problem. Those who refuse integration demonstrate that they are putting themselves beyond the bounds of true humanity.

Several aspects of the Graeco-Roman world have served to uphold this awareness that Christendom is established universality: the idea of a universal Roman Empire (ecumenical); the political monotheism of Byzantium, and its numerous avatars, which became actual Christianity with its European *elites* (and which still exists); the abstract universality of Greek philosophy and, hence, of Christian theology which is its legatee.

All this serves to maintain the idea that Christianity is universal by its very nature. This nature is not seen as particular to Christianity, but as the basic framework for the whole world. Christian theology is not regarded as a branch of thought, but as the only truly rational way of thinking. Christian law as a whole (divine and human, natural and positive, ecclesiastical and secular) is not a particular system of law, it is universal by definition. Christian existence is a complete cultural structure; one is a Christian because one has a place in this structure.

Under such conditions, missionary work is not really a challenge: there are no truly major obstacles to the integration of all men into the system. History lacks credibility, both for the Empire and for Greek thought; it will be found equally deficient by scholastic theology and Christendom as a whole.

4. UNIVERSALITY AND HISTORY

So it is history which presents the challenge today. In the aftermath of Vatican II, history is asserting itself. It has a Christian meaning, it is a constituent of eschatology and it excludes apocalyptism. It is not absorbed by Christendom, it is not at the disposal of that stable structure which is Christianity; it is actual and it questions both Christians and the Church.

Characteristically, the challenge of history has been apprehended and accepted not at the centre of Christendom, but on its periphery, by those people who had never been truly assimilated, who were better fitted to perceive the fragility of Christendom.

So, a living universality, in a state of permanent flux, is emerging in the face of an established, instituted concept of universality. Its principal characteristics are as follows.

(a) Christianity is not about knowledge or symbolisation, it is about life. To be a Christian is not to equip oneself with a wealth of learning or a structural framework, it is to live, to free oneself from whatever is at variance with life in order to be able to live life to the full. Jesus defined himself thus: the life, the way, the door, the bread, the light. He gives life, health, energy; he moves man to action. This is not merely a question of biological existence, nor of a reality alien to biological existence. It is a question of that vital dynamism for which every man, in his ardour for life, is responsible. Christianity is as universal as life, as death, as disease, hunger, fear, crying, anguish and hope; it takes hold of men at that level of existence which precedes their cultures, their mental or social structures.

(b) Christianity exists only in concrete terms, within individuals. It is not an objectification of all individuals in a great abstract reality beyond their experience. One is not a Christian because one adheres to Christianity, as though such a concept of Christianity existed. What does exist is the person of Christ and, bound to this person, millions of living individuals, all different, Christians by their very difference, each with his unique vocation, each one as a unique reality. The people of God is a fabric made up of unique pieces, joined together by millions of unique links. Universality in its multiplicity is as abundant as life.

(c) Universality is a state of perpetual activity: people opening out towards others, the active, reciprocal gift which comes from a feeling of concrete solidarity and which constitutes that solidarity. In radical terms, universality means destroying the distinction between friend and enemy. Once this distinction has been supressed, the gift prospers freely everywhere: consider the parable of the Good Samaritan, the unbounded forgiveness, the love of enemies and the meaningful gestures which Christ uses to convey the novelty of his message.

(d) This type of universality always follows a particular pattern: it begins and begins again. Its beginnings are quite specific. It begins with the poor, the outcast, the neglected, those who are of no account. It is the search for the lost sheep, for sinners, for publicans; these are the beatitudes. The beginning is Israel, the smallest and weakest race; it is Christ, a poor man, the Servant of God (Isa. 53); it is the Church of the humble and poor of Jerusalem or of Corinth. The gift of life goes where there is death, anguish; the gift of joy where there is sadness, and so on. True universality is among the poor, for they embody its essence and denounce those deceits which hide that essence, which is life.

(e) The universality of Christianity is the common cause of humanity: the liberation of the poor, the vast majority of people. Such a cause does not show itself in a straightforward political or ideological trend. It must be absorbed into thousands of correlated, interconnected individual actions, through which the poor themselves are called to be the authors of their own liberation. A task at once single and multiple!

If we keep to the viewpoint of Western Christendom, our task is: How to increase the number of Christians? And the challenge here is that the West seems to have reached an *impasse*. The West seems to meet with insuperable obstacles in the great cultures of the world: Islam, the Far East, Indian religions, African life.

One can skirt — in truth, ignore — the problem by relying on geo-politics: if China needs the West for the purposes of industrialisation, she must also open her doors to missionary activity; if the African states need Europe, they must give missionaries access to their peoples. That is to rely on the methods traditional to Christendom. But the question about Christendom remains: Is it made up of Christians or of adherents to political monotheism, Jesus' Pharisees?

If we enter on the path of liberation, people will firstly act as Christians, and this will lead them, one day, to develop an original witness of Christendom, independent of the old one. One day we will rediscover Paul's challenge to Peter in Antioch and in Jerusalem; Christianity will again be as varied in its manifestations as it truly is in its essence.

Finally then, the problem can be expressed in the form of two questions: (1) Is the judgement of God an event outside history, through a saving act which is outside history, or within history itself, as in Matt. 25:31-46? (2) Is history to serve the Church, to enable her to set up, little by little, a kind of Christian cosmos, a Christian summary of the universe in the guise of established Christendom, an instituted, concrete form of the universal; or is the Church to serve history, stimulated and questioned by it, ceaselessly 'converted' by the provocations of history, converted to serve the liberation of all men?

The Puebla conference gave a clear answer to both these questions: The judgement of God comes from within history, and the Church is to serve the cause of the full liberation of the poor. This constitutes her universality.

In the same way, the obstacles which presently confront missionary work are a call for conversion to true universality. All cultures, as well as Western culture, must be subject to the true judgement of God. Universality is on its way; it does not proceed from high-level agreements between representatives of the various civilisations, it proceeds by way of thousands of underlying, invisible channels and points of exchange.

Translated by Christine Halek

PART III

Some Major Implications

Anselme Sanon

The Universal Christian Message in Cultural Plurality

THE expression 'young Churches' is very relative, but it comes at once into sharp focus when applied to some Churches in Africa south of the Sahara. Can there be any other word for these Churches, most of which have not existed for more than 150-180 years? But is this recent origin in some way a point in their favour? We shall try to answer this question in terms of the cultural implantation of the universal gospel message (3), and in order to do so we shall examine the relations of the Church institution with African cultures (2) by looking at the existing communities (1).

1. WAITING OR PASSIVITY?

The episode in which the young David puts on Saul's armour and than takes it off before attacking Goliath has considerable relevance to the situation we shall be describing.

(a) The 'David' pastors

The bishops, pastors of the young churches and heirs of the missionary bishops, have received communities which, on the whole, are fervent.

These communities know the text of their catechism perfectly, but not always with the desired doctrinal foundation. They display a solid moral life, but sometimes lack the creative breath of charity which would prevent other failings. Faithful to their Sunday sacramental practice, they are satisfied with the received liturgical ritual even if it remains foreign to their domestic, family and social practice. On the contrary, they regard adaptation of the liturgy as unnecessary and a lessening of its dignity.

In general, compared with the first Christian communities of the years 95 to 150 A.D., ours do not go in for doctrinal quarrels. They are calm and peaceable Churches, showing little creativity. Clearly we are at the stage of assimilation and implantation (*Ad Gentes* 1-4), so much so that to say, like Vatican II (Decree on Missionary Activity, *Ad Gentes*, 22), that theological investigation is necessary in all areas seems to them little more than a stylistic flourish or a pious wish. In short, the security of the familiar makes them reluctant to change.

(b) *The impatient*

Faced with this situation, some people criticise 'the Church', by which they mean Rome and the Roman congregations, as the obstacle to movement.

In fact, even though the 'Roma locuta' image may remain, in their dealings with bishops, and in particular with the episcopal conferences, the congregations or the curia avoid the old style. Some documents may still betray a confused vision deriving from post-conciliar ecclesiology, but our obstacles are elsewhere.

First, exaggerations produced by the post-conciliar trend have alienated certain African bishops who were nevertheless council fathers. More important, however, is a sacral mentality which thinks in terms of objects rather than persons and is very strong in our communities: for example, communion in the hand was fiercely criticised and even rejected in some areas.

When these same communities show inadequate understanding deriving from an ignorance of the way the Church's tradition has evolved, and when a theoretical theological culture survives without seeking nourishment from the sources, it is clear that there will be many obstacles. In addition, the urgency of apostolic appeals, the many pressing tasks, the lack of organisation and the complexity of human relations at every level, all combine to make meetings, not times of reflection and study, but often enough of situation reports, based on particular solutions and exhorations but without any effort at theological or even doctrinal clarification.

Of course, lines of reflection have been opened up and are being pursued, but their pastoral impact remains slight. Impatience is understandable.

(c) *The successes*

As already mentioned, our communities can record one real achievement: the administrative personnel, though inadequate, exists and is growing in numbers. The hierarchy too has the joy of seeing ordinary

Christians with a firmly based faith. This progress of the faith is reflected in activities which have a real impact on the environment in helping to build a new society and a new style of relations with other beliefs and religions.

It is true that points of conflict still exist, with traditional religion, Islam and above all with modern society, which creates dynasties based on power, wealth and knowledge while disregarding many spiritual and moral values. Nevertheless a catechesis and a liturgy which are much closer to our educational needs are beginning to take shape, to the satisfaction of many.

(d) *Legitimate questions?*

In this context what is the meaning of a desire or quest for particularity within universality?

Does this concern come from pastors or scholars? Let us listen to the findings of the scholars.

(i) The traditional world

Even after leaving what we call the traditional ancestral world by choosing religion or modernity, we and our Christians are still immersed in this traditional mentality. Whether condemned or rehabilitated, this world knows that it represents a reserve of humanity for us, and that it provides fundamental points of reference for many people.

Indeed, newly baptised Christians in both country and town, of all levels of education, are, for various reasons, returning to this world and its practices. The reason is that they find there something they do not find in their new faith and that this faith does not satisfy all their needs, a sign that it is not well integrated. Those who return in this way to ancestral practices want to exploit them for their own benefit, but by so doing contribute to their maintenance and rehabilitation. Moreover, ideological and political tendencies such as authenticity, African dignity and socialism are also tending to have recourse, in one form or another, to this ancestral world.

The role of catechesis here is delicate.

The return of Christians to ancestral practices may mean, among town-dwellers, a return to the past or to familiar landmarks. It is a clear sign of the break, without integration, between the modern and traditional worlds. This striking gap between the rural environment and the modernity of the town means that townspeople cling to outward ritual practices without adopting their contents. What they are looking for is something they do not find in Christianity, areas where Christianity does not satisfy their needs. This is a sign of Christianity's failure to integrate.

(ii) The Moslem world

In sub-Saharan Africa and as far as the Equator, Islam is acquiring a new energy. In the ideology of the offensive Islam is the religion of the blacks and Christianity is a colonial import. Its power comes from money and petro-dollars. The result is political conversions and spectacular financial gains.

In such situations the Church must show great tact. As one organisation dealing with another, the Church often encounters suspicion and opposition, but these attitudes are not a response to the genuine spirit of the gospel or of the Council.

The confusion of politics and religion in Islam does not make things easier. Nevertheless catechesis must provide training in practical attitudes in inter-religious dialogue. This is the only appropriate attitude for believers who acknowledge one God and are obliged, by the extent of poverty and unbelief, to unite their faith and hope in the service of a world both materially and spiritually deprived.

(iii) The influence of modernity

The modern world, which in so many ways has shaken the grip of traditional societies, is increasingly influencing attitudes and actions.

It accelerates a first break with the social and natural environment. The effect of the new imported cultures have been to weaken the socio-cultural environment. They produce a different type of person who has not experienced the African's symbiosis with nature; on the contrary, this African, who has only a superficial knowledge of African humanism, wants to win technical control of everything. Nature is on the way to becoming a tool which he uses. The natural and social environment is disrupted for the sake of production rather than for consumption yet.

At the political and ideological level, and in reaction to the very recent colonialist legacy, these tendencies take the form of liberation movements, not only in politics, but also in economics and culture. One can sympathise with the slogan of the three battles, the third of which is for cultural independence: 'African authenticity is a complete revolutionary programme for political, economic and cultural independence.' Under the slogan of the rediscovery of authenticity there is an affirmation of the humanism of the New World of inter-cultural relations. Whether it is African, European or Asian, this intercultural humanism has its own legitimacy, without denying the others or questioning their validity.

In the case of Africa, there has been a realisation of the break with the ancestral world which has occurred. The African has lost his subjective and objective identity and has to rediscover it by trying to be faithful to his old traditions. Such a quest for cultural fidelity, wide-ranging at first, may prove ambiguous when faced with the problem of deciding what is and is not valuable in our traditions. As a result, political, economic and cultural decolonisation hardens into a political ideology which clashes with Christianity, which it sees as a foreign ideology, as power, and as a brake on emancipation. Here, therefore, we have a movement for a dynamic and lucid revival of indigenous values which challenges the universalist affirmation of the Church.

(e) *Where are our roots and our origins?*

It must be firmly stressed that the attempt to implant the Church's universality in particular cultures, especially African ones, is in no way a criticism of universalism but a requirement for faith deriving from the demands of cultures and implied in the incarnation itself. In other ways, universality as the Church's mission is based on the incarnation and has as its goal Paul's 'all things to all and in all', but its implementation includes a whole process which we cannot avoid today.

Historically, universalism or Catholicism has a centre which derives theological value from the demands of the incarnation. God became man by becoming man somewhere. That place is not a capital or a metropolis, a place of privileged faith (though it may be a privileged place of faith), controlling the periphery and imposing on it the conditions and norms of faith. It is a place where communion becomes more intense and where its horizon is the universe.

This means that universality is not diluted and then re-concentrated at need into exportable pills, manufactured products to be distributed with instructions. No, universality exists in the state of communion, which we may define as the sharing of the same function (*com-munus*), the same co-responsibility for universality.

If it is true that all our roots and origins are in the holy Church of God (Ps. 86), we have to find out how we can benefit from this.

2. INSTITUTION AND CULTURE

The Church as a collective undertaking made up of human beings is an institution. Is this ecclesial reality compatible with various institutional, social and cultural models? The answer of twenty centuries of experience is that the institutional model has varied. The important thing is to determine whether it is capable of that variability today, to the advantage of the individual churches. Does each individual church feel comfortable, at home, in the wider Church? To make this possible the Church must adequately reflect human diversity and, like a true mother, welcome all the elements of this diversity. Is she capable of being the mother of all cultures?

(a) *A limited view*

By virtue of its constitution, the Church is catholic (LG 8), universal, that is capable of being anything, capable of being essentially itself everywhere. It is the task of the institution to produce the best possible translation of this fundamental essence.

The experience of Western Christianity has been crucial here. The encounter of the Christian message and the Latin world was profound and fruitful in individuals, achievements and institutions which continue to influence human civilisation. This model, the model of Christendom, is in the eyes of many the ideal, the only valid version.

'Moreover, since all these institutional realities are regarded as a "datum" sent from on high and willed by God, we admire their uniformity and easily imagine that they escape from the cultural conditioning of a period or an area. To that extent we think of them as made for all men and human diversity is not taken into account' (Frisque, lecture notes).

Thinking of institutional realities as coming from on high and not part of the ordinary world and trying to maintain a universally valid uniformity, forgetting cultural conditioning, which is always the product of a particular period and area, and finally, not taking account of human diversity, all this is a temptation which none of us totally escapes. This is a limited view from which we must break out if we are not to distort the Church's encounter with other cultural and religious groups.

(b) *The shock of the encounter*

The encounter was not without collisions, and we are still experiencing sometimes unexpected repercussions, even within the Western communities (*Evangelii Nuntiandi*, 20).

In its overall tradition, African religious experience has always given priority to a whole spiritual dimension of its religious adventure. There were communal and ritual cultural institutions with the function of translating and protecting this dimension by means of primarily cultural events. On the other hand, the systematisation of religion took place more in ritual than in a body of doctrines.

A diagram, approximate as usual, may help to highlight the different emphases of the two traditions.

Traditional Religion	Emphases	Latin Christianity
	Systematisation	
−	doctrine (beliefs)	+
+	ritual (culture)	−
	Institutions	
−	social	+
+	cultural	−
	Spiritual Adventure	
−	individual (individuals in society)	+
+	collective (members of the community)	−

The thrust of Latin Christianity carries it towards doctrinal systematisation, social institutions and the individual dimension of belief, while African traditional religions, which are more inclined to collective experiences of the Spirit, manifest these in cultural and ritual institutions. In its encounter with other religions, Christianity is anxious to establish dialogue around a doctrinal corpus and to introduce social institutions. It tends to neglect the web of ritual which supports the collective cultural and cultic manifestations. Worship, culture and community are the pivots of traditional religion, and Christianity has failed to recognise this. However, a doctrine is easier to universalise than a rite or a cult. A social institution is easier to transpose than a cultural event, all the more because a cultural event is rooted in the hearts of the social group.

Christian universalism relies heavily on a doctrinal system, and therefore a doctrinal expression, and manifests itself in social institutions, for example, the celebration of the sacraments, but it has difficulties with ritual and worship, the cultural expression and communal dimension of spiritual experience. Converts, and non-Christians, even Moslems, readily adopt our relgioius language, but our liturgy lacks sparkle in comparison with traditional celebrations. Because traditional religion placed

G

religion on a human level, it accepts Christianity's universalising tendency and its attempt to systematise beliefs. On the other hand, traditional religion operated through culture, and here Christianity is vulnerable. Christianity on the one hand encouraged a breach between cult and culture and, on the other, socialised cultic rites. Immediately there was a danger that it would become a religion linked to a universal social pattern in which the universal doctrinal system, a conceptual structure, was detached from the demands of worship and the implications of culture.

Thus, in its encounter with traditional religions, Christian universalism forgot these three things:

(i) That it is built around a social model in which culture is merely implicit;

(ii) That it uses culture as a universal standard when in fact it is using a particular culture, that of the west;

(iii) That is has difficulty in recognising the unity and value of other cultures.

It is easy to see how Christianity could look like a religious system and how conversion was more like changing systems than changing beliefs.

(c) *Cultural Implantation*

In the course of time Christianity has lost its awareness of being implanted in certain cultural areas (Jewish meals, sacrificial rites, initiation rites, marriage rites), and has concentrated instead on their social equivalents, at a time when society was becoming secular.

This universalism by means of doctrinal, institutional and social systematisation, to the detriment of the cultural and communal dimension and to the advantage of a culture presented as a universal vehicle of faith, is the weak point of Christianity in its universal role. Without expecting Western Christianity to go into reverse, we can draw some useful lessons for the growth of the young Churches:

(i) Christianity is a universal religion;

(ii) Western Christianity is a valid version, but not normative on all aspects of this dimension;

(iii) Other cultural translations might find a place in the Father's house for the attention they would promote to rites of worship, the Christianisation of culture and the community expression of spiritual experience.

It is not a question of a choice between two versions of a prototype, far from it; but, in fidelity to the spirit of the incarnation and of Pentecost, the Church cannot call itself the one Church without accepting the demands of human diversity.

3. A NEW VERSION OF UNIVERSALISM

Through the redeeming incarnation, the Church is one, catholic, universal. Until now, it has had only one translation, the Eastern Churches. A new translation of the Christian message may be necessary in view of certain tendencies within the universalism of the Latin Church.

(a) *Universalism by induction*

Universalism is a gift of Christ to his Church (LG 8). Catholicity is the communion of all of us with our different gifts, in the unity of the same faith. Without going back to the scriptural sources, we can find this in the new ecclesiology of Vatican II.

What is new in this is the attempt at universalism by induction and not just by deduction. We are invited to join in a universality lived at the base, in local or individual churches, as a way of creating a new experience of universality which transcends all particularity. This places the Mediterranean or Western example in its context, recognising it as a valuable source of inspiration and in some points normative. Inductive catholicity will give priority to individual churches so that they can preserve their local character and an openness to their mission in the catholic communion. This was not always so, for many historical reasons. The universalism of the *universum,* of the *oikoumenē*, the inhabited world, was itself an affirmation of the ancient Graeco-Latin world, of the Mediterranean standard. The ecclesiastical or ecclesial order was envisaged at the time in terms of the West and the Mediterranean world.

The missions, the young Churches, entered this perspective as a simple extension of this network by accepting the faith. They were acknowledged 'laterally and incidentally', in H. Guitton's phrase. They received the universal Christian message in its western, Latin version, which was accepted as universal even in its cultural expression.

The Church's respect for all cultures is a frequent theme in papal documents, from the Instructions of 1659 to the first encylical of John-Paul II, but it is not so clear at the base that all attitudes of possessiveness, domination or condescension are rejected. An effort is being made today to think in terms of a total catholicity capable of accommodating the other cultures of the known world. We must therefore move from looking at others in an ethnological perspective to a true Christian anthropology. Faith and the Christian message can only be transmitted and received on the necessary basis of a culture and a cultural language. However, this is in no sense a transfer because it requires an act of exchange and communion.

(b) *A New Experiment in Universality*

The transmission of the message is essential to the survival of the Church (Mark 16). It consists of the celebration of the word and sacrament for the building up of the body of Christ.

(i) The transmission of the word

As Père Dournes has already shown (J. Dournes *Dieu aime les païens* [Paris 1963] pp. 129-50), the translation of the word into new languages and cultures in a form deeper than superficial equivalence results in a conversion which is a process of reciprocity at a very deep level between the transmitting language and the receiving language. Between the two, a whole reservoir of words, images and symbols is activated. This produces a biblical language for catechetical and liturgical use which in turn leads to the production of a theological language. We have already received vital clues from certain communities, in which the vocabulary of inter-personal and communal relations has expanded enormously.

Nor are the methods of transmission neutral. For example, the method of oral transmission can be used to memorise whole chapters of scripture. More important, there must be an abandonment of the Western systematisation which has extended the gap between catechesis and liturgy, doctrinal teaching and the practice of worship. We need a style which combines the best of both liturgy and instruction.

According to the new pedagogy based on *Gaudium et Spes*, the relations between the Christian message, especially in catechesis, and traditional cultures must be respected by the Church which, as Christ's human community, feels an inherent link with the spiritual journey of every human society. As a consequence of this, ministries serving the transmission of the message by means of the word will multiply, though the priest will remain the minister of the word in his community, not to monopolise it, but to ensure its distribution to all the ecclesial cells.

(ii) Transmission in liturgy and worship

We received the liturgical and sacramental tradition at the height of ritualism and of its canonical and doctrinal development. Apart from a few comparisons with the ritual of traditional religion, sacramentality and symbolism were presented more in their social aspect than in their cultural guise.

Where the adoption of local forms can hardly be avoided, as in the ritual of baptismal initiation and marriage, we are faced with the jungle of initiation rites and marriage customs on the one hand and the detailed prescriptions of Canon Law on the other. With the liturgy, in contrast, we begin to find that it is a celebration which can be enriched by local elements.

For all the talent of preachers in inculcating the duty of prayer, except for liturgical prayer, the experience of prayer will develop only slowly, through the communal approach of small groups.

Now, with regard to prayer, liturgy, the sacraments, i.e., worship in general, it is impossible to maintain that they are finished products, manufactured *en masse* to be dispatched throughout the Christian world with instructions to be deciphered by means of universal, uniform theological formulae.

This has as a consequence that universalism in our African communities must: first, take account of the cultural, and not just the social, dimension of worship and the sacraments; secondly, add to the doctrinal presentation of the sacraments their existential dimension: the Eucharist is a sacrifice, an offering and a celebration. In worship attention must be given to the community and its outlook, and, in the community, services rather than obligations must be fundamental; thirdly, see that the doctrinal systematisation is supplemented by the experience of a communal liturgical spirituality. There is a problem here in the relation of worship and culture. Does not the implantation of worship in a culture include the use of the fruits of the earth and human labour? How far is the use by Jesus of the fruits of wheat and the vine normative until the end of time?

(iii) Community organisation

Building the body of Christ and building the communities is one and the same thing. In the power of the resurrection the body and the Spirit are made for one another, by one another, in one another. Jesus gathers people together (John 11:50-51), as does the priest (Eph. 4:12), in order to build up the body by making it grow.

By what model should we build up this body, the Church? The only pattern is that of the Church today, the impetus given by Vatican II which is renewing our ecclesiology. The ecclesial model which came out of Vatican II is that of the Church as communion. 'Such a model, in our view,' says Frisque, 'must correspond to the language of communion.' If the Church is the people of God and the body of Christ, the emphasis will be on the person, with a consequent shift 'from the institution to the person'. 'The word is received as a mysterious reality which discloses itself to Christians in proportion to their faith and love' (Frisque). If the institution guarantees the unity of the Church and its catholicity, it cannot be 'like a reality which exists in advance of the language of believers'.

The institution cannot escape from human social, cultural and political history. Coextensive with the whole reality of the people of God, it will make every effort to sink roots in their diversity. It will encourage the birth of the fraternal body of Christ in cells of the Church which genuinely take account of socio-political and cultural pluralism. We must therefore seek and promote a unity of communion which is best able fully to respect diversity.

In this perspective the Church in upper Volta decided without hesitation in favour of a family Church. The bishops were well aware that the Church is the people of God (LG 9) and the body of Christ (LG 7), but from the many images contained in the Bible (people, body, bride, vine, family, flock) they selected that of the family (LG 6).

Such a decision, while not without precedent in the tradition, is unusual. On the other hand, given that every Christian family already is, or ought to be, a domestic Church (LG 11), it will be accepted that the experiment may be broadened to take account of a particular situation. An individual church, without closing itself off from the great universal tradition, can adapt itself to a particular situation which embodies universality in particular expressions. When I say that the Church is the family of God, I am repeating a traditional formula (LG 6), but if I ask what cultural embodiment this word 'family' implies I have gone beyond sociological analysis to a specific cultural experience. The idea of the Church as a society is more familiar than that of the Church as a community, and that of the Church as a family is even less so. When I say 'family', I am referring to a community, a society, a communion, horizontal and vertical relations and a whole tradition of sharing and communication in a particular tradition and pedagogy.

In what spirit should the community be organised? Despite our good intentions and our declarations, the Church appears not only as a hierarchical structure — which is normal — but also as one in which the hierarchy of command is more usual than the hierarchy of service. Now we know that, for Jesus, the hierarchy of fraternal service was primary (Luke 22:32 and Vatican II). This is the original feature in the community of Jesus, for in everything else the rulers of this world do the same (Luke 22:25).

On what cultural base does this hierarchical tradition of the Church rest? It rests on the idea of paternal authority, regarded as a universal phenomenon. In reality, other cultural traditions base authority on the maternal line (uncles and aunts) or on brothers. Christ's warnings come very close to this brotherly authority (Matt. 23:8-10; Luke 22:26-32; Vat. II: DS 3070). In good theology God is our father and Christ our master and our brother. All other office-holders in the Church are the servants of Christ; to us they are fathers, mothers and brothers all together (Col. 4:15; 1 Thess. 2:7) because of their responsibility in the service of Christ's gospel.

The way in which this authority and responsibility is exercised cannot be determined without cultural references, and universality must take this into account. Officials of the Church, when acting within communities or in dealings with other churches, must always remember that Christ is there and will return. This is the organisational principle of the community according to the spirit of Christ: the subsidiary criteria are those of translation into a cultural situation.

(c) *An African Christianity*

Pope Paul VI's injunction in Kampala, 'You must have an African Christianity' has remained an enigma on the horizon of African expectations. An African Christianity: for us this means an African expression of faith, its implantation in our particular cultures: first, in the area of thought and life, i.e. in theology in its full sense and in liturgy; secondly, at the level not only of social but also of cultural institutions, in the form of pastoral, catechetical and other research; thirdly, on the level of spirituality, making it more communal, giving greater weight to the structure of African sensibility (religious psychology and pedagogy). Will this mean a rupture within universalism or an opening out to root the message more firmly in particular societies? Three aspects claim our attention here.

(i) The cultural influence of the Christian message

The Faith is not neutral with regard to social and cultural life. It has an impact on them, uses them as a vehicle and acts on their development. The faith causes ruptures in social structures and sets off an intellectual reconstruction and finally a socio-cultural renewal which we could call economic and social development. This has a cost. To become implanted in this way in a culture means translating the universality of the Christian message which comes to heal and save the culture; consequently the faith can only express itself by using the instruments the culture offers it. As a result it shares the riches and limitations of that culture.

(ii) Redeeming cultures

The cultural identity of young countries is generally not recognised or respected by the international community. Few international or multinational programmes bother about it. The result is a politico-social and economic assimilation, reflected in the use of Western world languages and cultural models.

The Church's interest is not the same. In order to be acknowledged by the nations, the Church has an urgent duty to acknowledge them and to translate that acknowledgement into a base-level catholicity. This means that it must feel involved in everything which encourages the authentic cultural development of the nations who accept it.

(iii) The local church

Living catholicity in practice at base level must mean considering the local church. Vatican II's recognition of the local church is a novelty, a result of a renewed ecclesiology. Whereas whole churches could once be treated as though Christ the Lord were not present in them with his Spirit, Vatican II has already given the title of cells of the Church to family groups (LG 11), to the faithful gathered in the name of Christ (LG 26; SL 7; LG 8).

It is now becoming possible to see the local church as the embodiment of Christian communion at work in the life of a people and linked from within to that people's journey, while remaining a sharing open to the other churches in the Great Church. In short, the local church is the place where the universal message is implanted in a particular culture and the particular culture is ratified by the universal Church.

4. CONCLUSION OR HOPE

The implantation of universalism in particular cultures apart from the Latin or Western one is a legitimate demand, and is proving a difficult task, but it must be attempted, even if it involves risk, because it is not a luxury or a corollary of faith, but a necessity.

(a) The Christian universalism which derives from the universal character of the Christian message (Mark 16) does not come to destroy cultures, but to bring them a light of revelation which dispels their shadows and reveals, confirms and renews their inherent capacities.

(b) The universal Church, until now more concerned to give the faith a social dimension, will in future have to ensure its cultural implantation, since no true faith can exist except within a culture.

(c) The implantation of universalism is a task to be shared by the mind of the universal Church and that of the local church.

(d) The local church is the most favourable environment for expressing and translating the richness of the encounter between Christian universalism and the particularity of different cultures.

(e) In their attempt to express and translate the implantation of the Christian message into African cultures, the local churches, in fidelity to the originality of African religious traditions, will have to take account of the cultic and cultural dimension and the communal spirituality of the faith.

(f) In order to achieve a personal and communitarian transmission of the faith, the churches in African cultures will have to combine written and oral instruction, make use of presentation in images and symbols, and interpret the Christian essence in new forms.

Will these formulations and expressions all be consonant with the authorised language of the ancient ecclesial institution and will they be accepted within the theological or intellectual tradition of the Church?

(g) African theological scholars, obedient to the ecclesial experience of the communities, will have to show the inner unity of creation, including cultural creation and redemption.

Our hope for the Church of the second millennium is that it will learn to be the universal Church in a new — African — way in cultures in which it is such a recent arrival.

Translated by Francis McDonagh

PART IV
Bulletins

Ignace Puthiadam

Christian Faith and Life in a World of Religious Pluralism[1]

CHRISTIANITY entered India, the land of religions, already during the apostolic times. At least this is what tradition tells us. It is certain that from the fourth century Christians existed in India. Till the period of European colonialism, Christianity remained one of the religions of the land with little or no missionary thrust. The bishops came from the Middle East. The faithful themselves lived in harmony and peace with their Hindu brothers, accepting and following many of their customs, and exchanging gifts with them. Hindus and Christians often attended one another's feasts.

With the discovery of the sea route to India in 1498 and the beginnings of the colonial era in the 15th century a new 'type' of Christianity — aggressively missionary, convinced of its religious, cultural and even political supremacy came to the East. Already in 1454 Pope Nicholas V wrote the following lines: 'We, after careful deliberation and having considered that we have by our apostolic letters conceded to King Affonso the right total and absolute to invade, conquer and subject all the countries which are under the rule of the enemies of Christ, Saracens or Pagans . . .'[2] The Pope by the apostolic power possessed by him grants the sovereignty of the whole Orient 'in perpetutuum' to King Affonso and his successors. Thus the Christianity which came to the Orient with colonialism, was a religious organisation whose absolute claims had spread over and split into every sphere of human life and activity including politics.

After the first wave of Catholic missionaries from the various religious orders of the Church, there started the massive entrance of Protestant religious denominations. The Protestant missionaries were more evangelistic and conversion-minded than the Catholics. By the end of the

19th century wave after wave of missionary activity had swept over India and the east. Together with Christianity the missionaries had brought to the shores of the Eastern lands, foreign languages, European systems of education, liberal ideas of the West, works of corporal mercy, and a spirit of dynamism and conquest. They cultivated the languages of the people, helped the ancient peoples of the east to discover their own past literatures, religions and cultures. As far as the missionaries were concerned all their work for the people and the country of their adoption were subordinated to the prime purpose of their lives — the conquest of the Orient for Christ and his Church. Some of the missionaries studied the religions of the east and even adapted and adopted a few of their customs. They supported the colonial government's programme of Western educational schemes with a view to infiltrating the oriental societies, which were then considered to be in a process of dissolution. As one great Protestant missionary expressed the view, through Western education and the inculcation of the gospel Hindu religion and society could be exploded from within.

Most of the missionaries, with such rare exceptions as C. F. Andrews, were vocal and constant in their criticism of Oriental religions. From the moment St Francis Xavier penned the lines: 'The Brahmins are the most perverse people in the world and of them was written the psalmist's prayer: *"De gente non sancta, ab homine iniquo et doloso erue me"*— 'Were it not for these Brahmins all the heathens would be converted,'[3] till today, Christians have been on the whole negative and destructively critical of non-Christians.[4] A criticism without love, and a desire to root out the ancient religions of the Orient and in their place to plant Christianity, is till now the prevalent attitude among missionaries.

1. NON-CHRISTIAN REACTION TO CHRISTIANITY

It is with this Christianity, universalistic and absolute in its claims, firm in the conviction of its religious, cultural, economic and political superiority, openly or subtly missionary in its approach to non-Christians, that the Hindus have come into contact. This Christianity was at the same time engaged in the preaching of the dignity of man and human labour, ready to serve the oppressed, the exploited and the unwanted, efficient and thorough in the field of education, and highly organised and economically well off through foreign funds. Many of the modern and contemporary non-Christian servants have studied the Christian scriptures and even the growth of the various Christian Churches and their missionary methods. We do no know how the non-Christians reacted to the presence, life and practices of Christians before the advent of colonialism and the massive entrance of the Christian West into the East. But today we have innumerable reactions of non-Christians to the missionary movement that still goes on unabated in the East. Taking India alone for brevity's sake, we can say without any distortion of facts that the majority of the Hindus resent the Christian claims, the missionary activities and the way Christians show a certain contempt towards non-Christian religions. They are fighting for their traditions, religious and cultural identity and they consider the missionaries with their wealth pouring in from abroad, their hidden extra-territorial loyalties and aloofness a real threat to Hinduism's millenia long existence. Certainly in the opposition of the upper-caste Hindus to the Christian Churches apart from the legitimate attachment of their religion and traditions, there are also such elements as the desire to exploit the lower castes and tribals, to preserve the status quo and thus to perpetuate their dominance in society. Still even the best Hindus committed to the lifting up of the Hindu society and the suppression of all exploitation, do find the Christian claims unpalatable and unacceptable.

The Christian claim to universality and absoluteness is based on the faith that Jesus is the Son of God made man. 'It was more than I could believe that Jesus was the only Son of God and that only he who believed in Him would have everlasting life . . . My reason was not ready to believe literally that Jesus by his death and by his blood redeemed the sins of the world. Metaphorically there might be some truth in it . . . The pious lives of Christians did not give me anything that the lives of men of other faiths had failed to give . . . Philosophically there was nothing extraordinary in Christian principles . . . It was impossible for me to regard Christianity as a perfect religion or the greatest of all religions.[5] India's great philosopher-statesman S. Radhakrishnan is much more articulate and thorough in his rejection of Christianity: 'It is precisely this claim to absolute finality whether in the Church or in the Scripture or in Jesus Christ or in anything else, this claim that revelation belongs to a totally different order of reality than discovery . . . that perplexes and affronts those of us who have a proper sense of our own limitations.'[6] Gandhi writes: 'It would be the height of intolerance — and intolerance is a species of violence — to believe that your religion is superior to other religions and that you would be justified in wanting others to change to your faith.'[7] S. Radhakrishnan was convinced that 'the pathways we tread, the names we give, fade away into insignificance when we stand face to face in the glowing light of the Divine. When we touch the flame of the Divine a generous hospitality to different creeds and forms arises.'[8]

With the decline of the political power of the West in the East, the inner tensions inside the various Christian churches, the manifest break up of the religiosity of the Christians of the West and the exodus of Western youth from their Christian home lands into the 'pagan' East, the Christian claims appear to the non-Christians more hollow and less credible than before. The whole shift and change in Christian missionary theology and practice are watched with great interest by the Hindu and Buddhist thinkers. The failure of the Christian attacks on Hinduism and Buddhism left them stronger and more vigorous as a result of the adjustments they were called upon to make. In fact we find a resurgence in almost all the Oriental religions.

In spite of the non-Christian, chiefly Hindu resentment against the absolute claims of Christianity, the various oriental religions also affirm their own superiority. Swami Vivekananda and S. Radhakrishnan were conviced that Advaita Vendanta was the highest form of 'religion' fulfilling and completing all the lower grades of finite-infinite encounters. Gandhi applying his principle of *'swadesi'* (one's own country is best for oneself) believed that Hinduism was most suited to an Indian. From the time of the Rig Veda we find that each Indian subordinated all other beliefs and gods to his belief and god. In the Bhagavad Gītā, Krishna, the Supreme Being, subordinates faith in and worship of other gods to faith in and devotion to him. It is not true to say that the non-Christians accept that all religions are the same or are equal. 'All are equal but mine is more equal.' 'All are true but mine is more true'. This seems to be the attitude at least of the Hindus.

2. PAST AND PRESENT ATTITUDES OF CHRISTIANS TOWARDS NON-CHRISTIAN RELIGIONS

In the past many Christians have very negatively dismissed the non-Christians as the very children of the devil sitting in the shadow of death and waiting to be redeemed by the merits of Christ. Sometimes these men and women were looked upon as mere natural human beings bereft of all supernatural goodness and love. From the stand point of biblical revelation, non-Christian religions are mere unbelief and the work of human self affirmation and pride. True religion is only that event in the act of grace of God in Jesus Christ. In the present context of inter-religious communications and pluralist living the number of Christians who espouse purely negative attitudes to non-Christian religions and to their adherents is fast dwindling.

Other Christians both in the past and at present basing themselves on certain cardinal points of their faith as unfolded in the Old and New Testaments have taken a more positive attitude towards other religions. For a Christian, from the angle of his faith, the uniqueness and centrality of Jesus Christ in the salvific plan of God, God's universal will to save all men, the hidden and creative presence of the Holy Spirit at every time and place forming and fashioning the mystery of Christ in all men and the paternal providence of God towards all men of all times, are central in his approach to the theologically baffling and paradoxical mystery of the existence of non-Christian religions. Reflecting on these and other Christian faith-mysteries, theologians have spoken on the experience of the unknown Christ embodied in other religions; of the Christian seeds contained in them; of the non-Christian religions' function in the preparation of the nations to accept the fullness of the mystery of God in Christ; of the cosmic revelation embodied in the religions meant to be completed and crowned by the historical, deed — word revelation definitively achieved in the Christ-event. There are Christian theologians who believe that good non-Christians are anonymous Christians since Jesus Christ, as God-Man is the true and only efficient cause of our salvation; as the Son of God, he is our salvation itself and the access of grace to God the Father. Many Christian thinkers today hold the view that individual non-Christians in principle could be saved outside the visible communion of the Church. Still the Church represents and proclaims the love of God, gives testimony to hope and is a sign among the nations. But a couple of Christian thinkers reflecting on the present religious situation in the world have expressed the view that Christianity should be considered the extraordinary way of salvation and other religions the ordinary way. More and more Christians are ready to accept that genuine religious faith, real religious symbols and prophetic revelation could exist outside Christianity, that non-Christian religions have a salvific role to play in the life of their adherents. There are many things which Christians can learn from other religions. But at present no Christian seems ready to question the universality and uniqueness of Christianity since this community is the sacrament of that primordial and definitive encounter of God and men, Jesus Christ.

3. REFLECTIONS ON THE PAST AND PRESENT CHRISTIAN ATTITUDES

From the point of view of non-Christians almost all the Christian positions are 'reductionist' and 'integralist'. Ultimately they have the legitimate feeling that Christianity cannot really allow the *right* of religious pluralism. Since the fundamental Christian self-understanding posits itself as the salvation of the world in Christ, the other religions as socio-historical realities must accept Jesus Christ. They are no longer 'legitimate religions'. Some Christians might say that when Christianity is adequately and historically present, the other religions become obsolescent. 'Christianity understands itself as the absolute religion, intended for all men. It cannot recognise any other religion beside itself as of equal right.' As we read through these and similar statements of European and American Christians, we have the uneasy feeling that they only grudgingly accept the fact of religious pluralism. Theology cannot, given its

H

principles and sources find a real basis for the right of different religions to exist and to be equal partners with Christianity in dialogue.

The various theologies of non-Christian religions, except those which totally reject any salvific significance to them appear to a non-theologian creations of necessity. As we are more and more confronted with the fact of religious pluralism, which by no means can be overcome today (the semitic religions tried to do so even with the sword in the past), there arises the need to use theological ingenuity to find a way out of the difficulty. So what appears contradictory, is the attempt to join together a religiously monistic or totalitarian claim with pluralism, which by definition excludes it. This does not mean that *personal convictions, faith* as personal cannot be reconciled with pluralism. When personal convictions are universalised and absolutised, then pluralism has to suffer. So not one orthodox Christian theological position can defend fully religious pluralism, except in terms of freedom of conscience, which conscience unfortunately is in error, or imperfect, or implicitly and anonymously Christian.

In this context it is also instructive to see how theologians pick and choose scriptural texts to defend or reject one or other position. That we can find a clear teaching on pluralism in general or religious pluralism in particular in the Bible is certainly a most questionable proposition. That we need the Bible as the expression of the true Judeo-Christian experience, no Christian can deny. But that we can find normative solutions for the problems of our day in the Scriptures is a vain hope. But our solutions and even the search for them must take the biblical data into consideration, and on them we should test our efforts.

The Christian attitude to pluralism other than religious is more positive and dialogical. Many theologians have already written beautiful things about dialogue in a pluralistic society. They accept that dialogue has become the only possible mode of co-existence. So dialogue implies openness, self-criticism and the desire to learn. Each person enters into dialogue with his own convictions, yet without a priori subordinating the others to his convictions. Each partner is convinced that the expression of experienced truths are imperfect. Through silence the partners try to transcend what is expressed and reach out to the reality beyond words. These are all fine sentiments. When however a Christian encounters a non-Christian on the basis of religious faith, immediately there is a change in attitudes. The Christian is convinced that the *other* is not the *other* but an anonymous Christian, a man in whom, without his knowledge, Christ's saving grace is at work, a person whose religio-social cultural identity is not yet perfect, whose religious convictions as the result of the socio-religious reality from which he is born, through which he lives in which he will die have been truly abrogated in Jesus Christ.

These certainly are strong words. But the presuppositions behind the theological attitudes seem to warrant such statements. Can there be real dialogue in such a situation? Or is it a dialogue between the cat and the mouse? Both know the outcome of the dialogue beforehand. What is the common goal the dialogue partners are searching for? That both the sides can learn something from mutual exchanges is not denied. But can there be something substantial which the Christian can learn, from the *ray of truth* which *alone* others possess?

With one or two exceptions hardly any Christian theologian takes seriously the all-embracing providence of God and relates it to the reality of religions. It is easily accepted that non-Christian religions belong to the order of nature and thus to the general providence of God though inextricably mixed with error and sin. But the problem that troubles us today — it is for me a theological and nor merely a sociological one — is their continued existence and vitality. On the one side from a Christian dogmatic point of view, non-Christian religions have been radically abrogated. On the other for the last 2000 years, no other religion or not even the most powerful empires have spent so much money and men to convert the believers of other religions as Christianity. But yet on the whole the great religions of Asia and Islam not merely remain intact, but seem to be renewing and revitalising themselves. There was a time — the hey-day of western colonialism — when many Christians and some Asians believed that Christianity would soon make a final sweep of all other religions. But today the situation has radically changed.

Christianity does take seriously the differences of individuals. It is clear that inside the Church the same spirituality, or religious congregation cannot satisfy all men. The riches of Christ can be understood and lived differently according to the aptitudes and inner fitness of each Christian. If this position is pushed further we might legitimately ask the question whether it is in the providence of God to put all the peoples of the world into one religion, however rich it may be. It is by its very historicity finite, conditioned, growing. Both the history of religions, the present pluralism of religions and the tenacity with which individuals and groups cling to their religions seem to indicate that God wants religious pluralism. The same God who wants the individuals to be different, groups and nations to grow in their own separateness, seems to want also religious pluralism. We cannot just argue here that non-Christian religions are existing out of God's sufferance, or as a result of men's concupiscence and hubris. There is a unity and tremendous diversity among men. This diversity calls for socio-religious realities in and through which they can express their different and original experiences (God's revelations) and aspirations.

Moreover we should take the inner unity and pluralism in the life of God as the Christian doctrine of Trinity teaches or as the Hindu doctrine of God's many-sidedness and thousand names indicate very seriously. This doctrine together with the teaching on man's individual and group differences have tremendous repercussions. It does seem to be unwarranted to affirm that unity would be established at the end of times. 'Pluralism' stamps reality; not brute plurality but the harmonious union of infinite riches. Pluralism of *ultimate* experiences of that one yet many faced or triune God will characterise man's eschatological state too. Eternity too would be the harmony of opposites, unity in diversity.

4. TOWARDS A THEOLOGY OF NON-CHRISTIAN RELIGIONS

The first requirement for a genuine theology of non-Christian religions implies that we Christians should not arrogate to ourselves and to the Church the absoluteness which Jesus alone possesses. It is true that on the meaning of Jesus' absoluteness we need further theological reflection stemming from a transreligious experience. But for the time being let us concentrate our attention on our own claims. Claims like: 'Outside the Church there is no salvation'; literal interpretations of words like 'Truly, truly, I say to you, unless one is born of water and Spirit, he cannot enter the Kingdom of God' (John 3.5) (interpreted at first to mean actual baptism) or 'Unless you eat the flesh of the Son of Man and drink his blood, you have no life in you' (John 6.53) (interpreted to mean actual reception of the eucharist) have produced a false sense of definitiveness, absoluteness and condescending mentality in Christians. From history we know how the interpretations of these texts changed in course of time, when facts were seen not to fit in with claims, though we were clever enough to find such distinctions as 'implicit and explicit', 'unthematic and thematic', 'votum' and 'in re'.

Christianity's, the Church's and her message's claim to absoluteness and definitiveness from the time of Constantine till recent times, also meant special relationship to the state. But let us not enter into this complicated history, though it has many lessons to teach us on our problem. But the fact is that Christianity, to whatever ecclesial community the missionaries belonged, was stamped with a false pride, sense of superiority, ignorance of other religons and with a proneness to relegate others to an inferior position. Even as recently as 1939 Pius XII recalling the decision of Benedict XIV could not accept that the Chinese rites were religious. Officially it is Vatican II that finally declared: 'The Catholic Church rejects nothing which is true and holy in other religions.' 'She looks with sincere respect upon those ways of conduct and life, those rules and teachings which, though differing in many particulars from what She holds and sets forth, nevertheless often reflect a ray of that Truth which enlightens all men.' Compared to the past pronouncements a very generous profession indeed! But certain questions arise: These differing ways — do they contain some truth which the Church does not possess? Or do these religions possess only a share in the truth which the Church possesses fully or in the highest possible degree?

In the Roman Synod of 1974 Mgr. Tashibangu claimed that Christian theology has the right to invalidate, corroborate, correct and extend non-Christian beliefs. This is a common Christian attitude that claims the right to sit in judgement on the faith and practice of others. From all what we have said, we want to draw the conclusion that if we alone possess the right to choose the criteria of religious encounter, that if we alone can really distinguish right and wrong, values and non-values we cannot be just to others.

It is quite legitimate that in our inner ecclesial ecumenism, we can as a shared faith profess that all the Churches are converging towards Christ. Here each Church questions the absolute claims of the other Churches; but all can agree on the absoluteness of Christ. When we move out into the wider field of religions, they question not merely Christianity's absoluteness but Christ's. If intra-ecclesial ecumenism has to be genuine and dialogical, then each Church from its faith and practice has the right to question and probe the faith and practice of the other.

In a similar way if the Christian has the right to question and judge the believers of other religions in the name of the gospel, they too have the equal right to question and judge my faith and life in the name of his religion. Unless we can cultivate the courage to take the other as the other, the Scriptures of other religions as they are and not as 'pre-Christian', and the non-Christians as genuine Hindus, Moslems, Buddhists and not as anonymous Christians, or imperfect beings non-thematically desiring fulfilment in our religion, we cannot create a theology. As we shall see theology springs from life. So the theologies created by us up to now from our Christian isolation, from purely inner Christian presuppositions have not really touched the facts. The self identity of each religion has to be sought by us. We have to let it be revealed to us by the religions themselves. So we need a real understanding of other religions in all charity and truth.

To go a step further I as a Christian believing fully in the God who came to me in Christ must show myself ready to accept that my non-Christian brothers too possess absolute centres in their lives and religions. Each religion believes and proclaims absolute centres. But the whole problem is: Can two or more 'absolutes' co-exist? We are on the level of faith, of life, i.e. in a state of pilgrimage, of ongoing process. Our faith is not fixed in a static but 'moving absolute'. Secondly, the attitude and conviction of superiority, the belief that the total truth is with us are contrary to genuine pluralism. But can my faith, my convictions and the centre of my faith and the faith-convictions and centre of belief of the other be linked to the idea of otherness, or relationship? This is not an 'a priori' question which we can settle by thinking on some abstract principles, but a practical question that must be answered by means of a new life. Two persons are related but not relativised by one another. Christian theology of the Trinity of persons may throw some light on this proposition. This implies that ultimately 'religions cannot be graded as inferior and superior, or reducing and reducible'. They are linked together like all realities by otherness. As other they are related.

Religions are not God. They are human though necessarily related to an absolute centre. What are they in God? This is beyond our ken. But as human realities, even as revelations, 'however absolute they may be, that is to say, unsurpassable in regard to their essential assertions or negations — they remain finite and inter-related by their otherness, they are partly similar, partly complementary, and partly antagonistic to one another. Each one brings an absolute point of view: absolute because it is unsurpassable; a point of view because no revelation can express the totality in human language, since man is never totality and never of a piece. That is why relationship between the religions emerges as one of action-reaction.' Since religions belong to the symbolic domain, they function as symbols, and it is only structurally that symbols are meaningful. 'It is only in accordance with structural oppositions that religious absolutes are meaningful. The Christian trinitarian affirmation is meaningful only in relation to the Islamic affirmation of the divine oneness; pantheistic affirmations are meaningful only in relation to the distinction between God and his creature; the African religious affirmations, centred on the essential needs of the human condition becomes meaningful only when they are structurally opposed to the affirmations of the prophetic religions in which God manifests himself to men with his very own projects. These contrasting affirmations can no more cancel one another than the day cancels the night or vice-versa. That is why the religions must witness to themselves, in their diversities, so that they may assume their full meaning.'[9]

Maurier has expanded and defended his position by means of three biblical paradigms. The God of the Bible though absolute, superior to all, never suppresses man. Man is a partner in the Covenant. Between God and man there is the relationship of friends, or husband and wife, one not suppressing other. The union of divinity and humanity in Christ is also not one of suppression or absorption. So too nature and grace do not destroy one another.[10]

In these paradigms the point of comparison is the respect one has for the other; one letting the other exist. What is hinted at is that Christian revelation can give us a ground for understanding the possiblity of accepting the other as the other. As it was often said, theology, genuine, creative theology can arise only from real Christian life. What is called for in India is a new life. By this new life I mean a 'trans-cultural and also a trans-religious life'. First of all, I must try not to be limited by the culture in which I grew up. I try not to be bound by a limited set of values, of world views and or problems. I do not try to be aggressively apologetic. In my flesh and blood I try to live, as far as my abilities allow, the culture, the world-views, the problems of others, without giving up my faith, the glimpse of truth God has granted me. Of course I will see and experience in my life similarities, complementary elements and antagonisms. I will find in the other, (for the non-Christian religions, cultures are not abstract, disembodied realities but real concrete men living the religions and cultures) otherness, irreducibility. I will accept and search further into that Mystery where I and he meet and through whom both of us are related. This brings into my life integration, catholicity and the understanding that both he and I are on a common pilgrimage. I do not put a prophetic history-centred religion on a higher pedestal at the expense of a more mysterical, experience-centred and less history-oriented religion. In my life I will try to bring them together with their real otherness and yet mutual relatedness founded on *God* who is far beyond all the *absolutes* of the religions as socio-psychological and historically conditioned realities.

When I began the serious study of Indian religions, Christian theology, liturgy and spirituality hardly took non-Christian religions and their riches and the religious identity of non-Christians into consideration. Christian theology of non-Christian religions remained with such theories as 'fulfilment' and 'anonymous Christianity'. Into liturgy no one thought of introducing non-Christian Scriptures. Indian spiritual methods and insights did not play a role in Indian Christian spirituality. But as time went by Christianity became more and more positively aware of non-Christian religions. As I entered more and more deeply into the understanding of the non-Christians' experience of 'God' as emboided in their texts and life, new religious 'attitudes' and 'feelings' arose in me. The manifoldness of God's faces took firmer root in my heart and mind. Some of the Rg-Vedic hymns revealed to me a 'cosmic liturgy'. Nature in its grandeur and splendour is not *merely* the 'handiwork of an omnipotent and loving Father'. In nature and its great phenomena, I began experiencing aspects of the Infinite Absolute Ground in which all live, move and have their being. From many of the Old and New Testament passages and from the study of Christian philosophy and theology I had learnt and to some extent experienced the 'creatureliness of nature', and 'man's duty of dominating nature'. A few of the Rg-Verdic hymns, passages from the Upanishads, Gītā and above all the writings of Hindu saints brought me face to face with the 'godliness of nature' and with my duty to discover its sacredness and to 'serve nature'. Nothing has brought home to my inner-most consciousness the experience of the bridging filament of joy and 'divinity' running through and uniting God-Man-Nature as the texts of some of the middle and later Upanishads, the Bhagavad Gītā and the writings of Hindu saints. In the Christian experience I do feel the actuality of the I-Thou relationship, my and man's sinfulness and above all man's uniqueness (distraction from God and nature). Yet the non-Christian experiences made me enter into the paradoxical awareness that at the very interiority of this *bheda* (distinction) there is a running thread of *abheda* (non-distinction) which I cannot adequately explain by the category of 'presence' I had studied in philosophy and theology. I have an inkling that the meaning of the phrase 'immanence of God in man and nature' is more than *intimior intimo meo*.

Christian views of creation, I-Thou relationship, personalism, without losing their sharpness, entered into a relationship of complementarity and otherness with the non-Christian experiences of oneness, absorption, a relation transcending personality. All these experiences though con-ceptually and logically exclusive seem to merge in actual life into a coincidence of opposites, of unity in diversity, of *bheda-abheda*.

5. REFLECTIONS OF MY EXPERIENCE

My first reflection centres round the problem, significance and function of 'difference'. Any honest man faced with the world must accept the reality of difference. Christians have attempted philosophically and theologically to found, explain and praise differences. Difference is the rule of life: sexes, races, cultures, material things, God and man, God and nature, men among themselves, men and nature. In fact we accept dif-ference even within the very interiority of God. Differences are signs of the richness of an underlying mystery; they are complementary, mutually enriching and pointing to a ground and goal beyond. Yet each religion instinctively constructs a theology of other religions, which does away with differences. The different attitudes of Old Testament people to the 'pagans' around them and the attempt of Krishna to proclaim a sort of anonymous Krishnaism in the Gītā are examples of this preoccupation. The way in which one sect within Hinduism tries to subordinate the other sects to itself is indeed revealing. Modern Hinduism is of the 'absorbent type'. All religions are the same. They say the same thing in different words. But in persons like Vivekananda and Radhakrishnan we can detect a tone of superiority. In these aborbent theologies there is a conscious or unconscious effort to bypass differences.

Others — the exclusive types — try to reduce and annul differences by insisting that their religious experience (scriptures) is 'normative', complete, definitive. By various combinations of the ideas of 'fulness', and 'parts', 'one-pointedness' and 'ambivalence' together with the notion of 'conversion', they try to bring about unity. These theologies in whatever form they may appear ultimately question the real validity of 'religious difference'. Thus both the classical Christian theologies of religions and modern Hindu thought seek to suppress ultimate religious differences.

The ultimate mystery experienced by all religions and expressed in the sacred texts is the same; but the manner in which God is experienced and expressed is different. It is the other as other that complements me. To deny the otherness of religions is to deny truth.

In every religion as it is lived, sin and grace play hide and seek. Even the very founding experience of religions is a combination of the eruption of the divine and the resistance, fallibility and receptivity of man. Instead of constructing absolute 'apologetics', we could accept the principle of otherness, of complementarity, of mutual enrichment and fulfilment, in the area of religious pluralism. All genuine religious experiences are moving towards the inexpressible mystery of God. As a Christian I would say that that God is the God who came to me in Christ, though I am quite conscious that he can come to man in any form he likes — myths, persons, etc. God can raise up children unto himself from the very stones!

This principle will raise many problems: evangelisation, salvation in Christ alone etc. I have no ready-made answers to any problem. Still without doubt or question Christians must witness to their genuine religious experience and truth. But the other religions have equally the right and the duty to bear witness to their religious faith and life. Mission implies also the establishment of communication and communion with the believers of all religions by means of genuine dialogue. Conversion as a free passage from one centre of meaning and identity to another is certainly accepted. This way of conceiving the mission will change its traditional face. It is no more an expedition to conquer and convert all men. It is a humble witnessing of our faith and letting others witness to their faith to us. It is a process of mutual growth in and pilgrimage to the Source and Goal of all men and history.

My second reflection is on the contingency and finitude of every historical word and event. I have the doubt and the fear whether any 'historical event' can be the fulness of 'God's self manifestation'. Of course the Risen Christ transcends history. But is not the Risen Christ more a 'pointer to the Mystery beyond'. I find in every sect of Hinduism, in Buddhism and Jainism 'sacramental reality' enclosing and pointing towards an absolute and ineffable Mystery. Since God speaks to us in our tongues, in accordance with our geographical, historical and cultural situations, his self-revelation will go on till the end of times. Perhaps we may say that one aspect of his self-manifestation — the Judaeo-Christian, world-event, election-goal oriented, historical revelation is completed in Jesus. Besides this and the cosmic revelation is there not the possibility of God manifesting 'his faces' through persons, things and myths, each unique in its own order? each absolute in its own manner?

Notes

1. This article is written from an Indian Christian theological angle and mostly touches on the religious pluralism of the Indian subcontinent.

2. Quoted by K. M. Panikkar *Asia and Western Dominance* (London 1959), p. 27.

3. Quoted by V. Cronin *A Pearl to India* (New York 1959), p. 84.

4. The word 'non-Christian' though more polite than infidel, heathen or pagan is still negative. The adherents of other religions are still understood and termed in relation to Christianity. Since I do not have a more precise and better term, I am forced to use it in this essay.

5. M. K. Gandhi *Christian Missions, Their Place in India* (Ahmedabad 1941), pp. 24-25.

6. S. Radhakrishnan *Recovery of Faith*, p. 195.

7. M. K. Ghandi *The Harijan* (May 14, 1938).

8. S. Radharrishnan *Occasional Speeches and Writings (May 1962-May 1964)* pp. 178-179.

9. H. Maurier 'The Christian Theology of Non-Christian Religions' *Lumen Vitae* No. 1 (1976) 72 and footnote 12.

10. *Ibid.* pp. 72-74.

Anon.*

Jerusalem: Some Reflections on a City that is 'Unique and Universal' for the Monotheistic Religions

1. REVELATION

IT IS not easy to recapture the inaugural and constitutive data of a living tradition and to formulate them in a systematic discourse: 'origin' is here tantamount to 'originating', or, in other words, to some proto-phenomenon transcending any later interpretation. What this entails, for those who have eyes to see, is that the meaning of the origin is always available to be tapped and caught anew. We are no doubt probably right to insist that it is the way in which Jerusalem[1] figures in the respective revelations of the three great religions that makes it at once quite so unique and universal. It is for this reason that these two aspects are beyond question.

Abraham, The First Passer-by

This 'man of all beginnings' came into contact with Jerusalem as it was being born. This was an originating event but it did not mean that either one or the other was taken over by any one of the three traditions to the exclusion of the others. On the contrary, it meant that they are involved in it together, or, even better, find it in a focus of communication.

So far as Judaism is concerned, we need hardly recall that it sees in

*The author is professor of comparative religions and epistemology in a university and is a member of the Orthodox Church. He prefers to retain his anonymity on account of the exploratory nature of these reflections and because his work and connections keep him at the very centre of the confrontations still being played out between the three great religions which are the subject-matter of this article.

Abraham the initiator of the adventure of faith through his act of simultaneously leaving everything and abandoning himself to God's unpredictable claim upon him. He remains quite clearly the emblematic Father,
the undeniable and living proof of the faith of the Hebrew people. Even
when he had established himself ethnically in Palestine through the
occupation of the 'promised land' by conquest and the first fruits of the
produce of the soil had been brought in offering (and we know the
symbolic resonance of this gesture of integration that is at once cosmic
and sacral), the tutelary presence reasserts itself: 'And you shall make
response before the Lord your God, "A wandering Bedouin was my
father . . ."' (Deut. 26:5). In other words, Abraham's journeying is a
'being called in faith'. This journey has its stages, it meets obstacles and it
contains pauses, but what is special about it is the urge to press on beyond
all this. This is high-lighted by that summons from even higher above
which denounces every form of settling down, every attachment — even
to his only son Isaac — and to which the same Abraham, on Mount
Moriah, replies: 'Here I am.' So there are two terms — 'Go . . .' 'Here I
am' — to the break (which will be mended only with the consummation of
the last time, for it is the spring of new life, from God to man, from man to
God), and between them Abraham keeps watch as our universal intercessor: 'Father of all believers.'

And these last remarks take us to the space which the Islamic tradition
made to welcome the universality of Abraham. This space has not
received much attention in theological reflection properly so called and
the exploration of it has been largely confined to specialists and to people
on the edge of things . . . And because the sense of evolution through time
has now been well and triumphantly established by the other two traditions, it is the case that, practically wherever it is studied, the Islamic
anchoring 'in the faith of Abraham' is seen as something of a religious as
well as a temporal regression. And conformism reinforces this tendency.

Now, for those who hold it, the Islamic vision of Abraham does involve
a return, but a return to something in the nature of a revelation made
precisely through Abraham as a locus.[2] This could be the reason why he is
at once so sharply defined and so limpid. We can sum this up very briefly.
In the words of the Qur'an (2,48) Abraham 'was neither Jew nor Christian, but a *hânif*,' a pure *believer*. This is why he was and therefore remains
(3,60) the *Imam* (the guide, the one who orientates) of all pure believers.
This is Abraham's essential prophetic function, and Islam's specific task is
to bring this fact back to light. This has two corollaries. The Muslim faith
cannot but exclude the exclusion of other faith communities that are also
founded on Abraham. And it does this very positively, since the 'Father of
all believers' already gathers them together in the sense of the faith to
which he witnesses (using 'sense' here in its double meaning of direction

and communication of significance); they are included in the *Ahl-al-Kitab*, the 'community of the people of the Book', each in their own place.

We have to trace the rise and development of this line through and 'between' phases of history, even at a distance. And there is all the more reason for doing so in that from the very beginning this line crossed the site of the place we have referred to as naissant Jerusalem. This is what gives the city its fundamental topology and outlines the permanently revealing significance that establishes the measure of the city's fidelity to itself in the design of God as well as of the fidelity of the faithful who will 'turn' to it in order to locate themselves by reference to it.[3]

And this is also precisely where the Christian horizon over the naissant Jerusalem emerges.

It is situated below (or above) the realm of quantifiable history. All that the latter can do, usually, is to frame hypotheses about the identification of a site with the future Jerusalem of the Bible. It is called 'Salem', which is a significant enough place-name, on its own account and on account of what it says, 'Peace': 'And Melchizedech king of Salem brought out bread and wine; he was priest of God Most High . . . "who has delivered your enemies into your hand!" And Abram gave him a tenth of everything.' (Gen. 14:18-20).

The city where 'God's name will reside' must be approached, without any play on words, as a 'non-place', beyond any individual or collective self, the inaugural celebration of a new Love. In fact the Christian faith will rediscover in the cross of Christ the cipher of the World who was with God in the beginning and whose self-abandonment (*kenosis*: Phil. 2:7) even unto death 'speaks' the love of a God who first loved us: the vision of a 'Jerusalem, city of Love' very probably finds one of its rare but unassailable confirmations here.

A Kingdom in Jerusalem. The By-product of the Temple

These first foundations of Jerusalem, high-lighted as they are by revelation, will inevitably serve the building of the historic Jerusalem which throughout its complex development will never cease to refer to them. At a typological level which is also valid for the other religious traditions that issued from Jerusalem, such, for example, as Christianity, Jerusalem seem to be caught in a tension between, on the one hand, a theocratic tendency and, on the other, liberating upheavals that look *back* to the original vocation as much as *forward* to its eschatological destiny. It exhibits the structure of the basic antinomy which is insoluble as long as history lasts, for it marks the very duration of history, caught as it is between the 'Jerusalem that is above' (heavenly) and the 'Jerusalem that is below' (earthly). We know the stages of the unfolding of the latter in virtue of the double principle of the state (the 'throne of David') and of religion (the 'temple'). When David transfers the ark of the covenant there from Kireath-jearim, he 'transforms Jerusalem from a Canaanite sanctuary into a city consecrated to God, the political and sacred centre of Israel, a capital city the status of which as such could not be justified on either geographical or economic grounds'.[4] The primitive 'Canaanite sanctuary', which is probably represented by the first stratum detectable under all those that followed, belonged to the Jebusites, whose name figures 'in the list of people wiped out by Israel'.[5] For ambivalence made its appearance here to an extreme degree. To want to deny or suppress this fact would virtually amount to wanting to efface the concrete reality of this town, to the point of reducing to a simple metaphor the truth of the denunciations which the prophets made against this Jerusalem by contrasting it with another. It is true that the 'holy city' is not spared the universal fatality and evil of wars, but does it not, from the loftiness of its future, preside over the systematic setting in motion of what we have to call 'sacralised genocide'? The way in which the conquest of the space destined to supply its base ('holy land') is carried through is perceived as a right or duty stemming from the monotheist exclusiveness inserted into the course of history and overshadowing peoples' freedom (Deut. 20:10-17; Joshua 6:20-21 and 24:13).

Does this signal the appearance of a new 'model of universality', a universality of extension, on the basis of the 'power and the glory' (at once doctrinal and material) of a 'centre'? This is a fascinating question which will recur right down the centuries of Western civilisation. Let us content ourselves with noting here, in passing, how much the future institution of 'wars of religion' especially in the west and even after its secularisation, refers back for its justification to the original model of this enterprise conducted in the shadow of Jerusalem . . .

The themes and issues are complex and they hide the perpetually surprising significance of the conjunction of Jerusalem with the temple. What is in question here is the 'scandalous' possibility of seeing a certain sort of idolatry arise from the very heart of Abrahamic monotheism. And this occurs not through some contamination from outside but as a logical by-product of the sense transmitted in revelation. We can start by recognising that it has taken us time in our culture to begin to understand the naivete of the terrifying catalogue of 'idols' drawn up as an indictment against 'pagan', archaic, primitive religions . . . What underlines the difference between the divine and the human is the very materiality of the sacral object, a crassness so hard that is sometimes suggests cosmic minerality, and it does this without having recourse to an interpretation in terms of symbol and hierophanies which tends to detract from this very heaviness. The graven 'idol' does not confuse the divine and the human;

on the contrary it rather represents the distance between them. The way that idolatry returns to the very places where uniqueness of God is declared is subtly different. For these 'places' and, with them, God who speaks there — seem to allow themselves to be appropriated in their very exclusiveness: kept for 'me' alone to the exclusion of others. The distance between the unique God and his faithful is forgotten in the 'religious' and institutional turn of events which defines the distance of monotheism in terms of excluding others. The 'Jerusalem' which, as we have seen, functioned to orientate the space of Abraham's faith condenses into a token of 'divine identity' which is appropriated by some to the extent that it is fused with the 'divine' expropriation of others. This is more or less the way that Gregory of Nyssa in the fourth century described the sliding of faith towards an 'idolatry of the true God'. The appeal which the prophets then make is like an exorcism, and they refer to an innominate Jerusalem, the 'visitor'. The earthly city is seen in spirit as idolatrous: Sodom and Egypt (Rev. 11:8), regions essentially inhospitable towards the visitation of God and the freedom of man. And on the dawn of Easter morning Luke's account welcomes the return of the risen one as that of the 'only visitor to Jerusalem' (Luke 24:18).[6]

The Nocturnal Ascension of the Prophet

Jerusalem, under both its aspects as 'earthly' and 'heavenly' is far from being absent from Islamic revelation itself before becoming part of the history of Islam. The mere fact is already pregnant with meaning. The relevant passage of the Qur'an reads like a visionary account. The text takes for granted the traditional significance of the holy city, for its temple may have been abolished at the time but the meaning remained because it was based on the atemporal 'anteriority' of the model 'on high'. It is towards this place that the 'stranger' 'of the line of the faith of Abraham' is transported by night from his Arab sanctuary after having symbolically touched the site of the temple. 'Glory to him who made his servant travel from the sacrosanct temple (al-masjad al haram, of Mecca) as far as the furthermost temple (al-masjad al-agsâ, the temple of Jerusalem) on which we have placed our blessing, in order to enable him to see some of our signs' (Qur'an 17,1). Following on from the nocturnal journey (isra) from Mecca to Jerusalem, the text then goes on to describe the nocturnal ascension properly so called (mi'râj) by Gabriel's side through the seven heavens opened up through the 'gate of the city' Jerusalem. Gabriel is asked his name and that of his companion, Mahomet, in front of the door of each of the seven heavens before Mahomet meets the prophets who had been sent before him and identified himself to them in his own turn.

We do not here need to recall the different levels of possible interpretation of this fundamental text of Islam. What we do need to do, however, is to understand just how extraordinarily coherent the image of Jerusalem finally becomes. What we have to do with in the first place is a scene of initiation and prophetic investiture of the new 'emissary of God' (*Rassul-Allah*) who finds it incumbent on him to go via the materially significant place of Jerusalem in order to proceed on from there to the epiphany of the 'heavenly' city. What has not been noticed so much, although it is decisive for the understanding of Islam, is the critical acknowledgement here of a *prophetic pluralism*. The 'last of the prophets', Mahomet, does not intend to cast the others into oblivion; on the contrary, he goes up towards them in order to have himself accredited within the divine scheme of which they were the legitimate heralds. They are greeted as such. Now this 'universality' in the prophetic spirit can take place only in 'Jerusalem above' which is already actively present. The most that Jerusalem 'below' could do would be to lead to it through a transparency that it can never ensure itself. For this transparency is nothing else (and this is the third meaning of our text) than uprightness, keeping steadfastly *oriented* towards the heavenly Jerusalem. And it is only through keeping the eyes of faith open in this way that the 'holy city' deserves its dignity as 'first *qibla*' ('*aula al qibla theyn*', Qur'an 2, 136: the first of the two *qibla*, the other being Mecca). The Muslim tradition also calls it the East, the place of the rising sun, by way of contrast with the earthly world which it sees as the West, the place of the setting sun.

This is a literally crucial situation which enables us to understand why for the Christian faith and despite its important historical moorings, the basic meaning of Jerusalem is to be seen not so much in a Christological as in a pneumatological horizon.

The Coming of Christ. The Descent of the Spirit

We have to unite the two moments of a single revelation. This could involve challenging certain received ideas. For does not Jerusalem spontaneously conjure up the long-established imagery of devotion to the holy places where Christ lived and was crucified? Are pilgrimages not organised, are currents, if not institutions, of piety not kept up in his name? Is the 'holy city' not criss-crossed with stations and routes which are often transposed into the religious practice of the Christian West (even if we persist in calling the place which according to the earliest traditions was simply called the *Anastasis*, resurrection, 'Holy Sepulchre'?).

It is certainly not in this Jerusalem, constructed as it is out of uncertain elements of the psyche and religious customs, that we are going to seek out the true significance for the Christian faith. This is to be found, fundamentally, in the 'person' of Christ himself: locus, knowledge, epiphany of the mystery of God himself. Scholars of the New Testament have not failed to point out how little importance attaches to the city of

Jerusalem thought of as the cultural site of the covenant and the concrete symbol of the politico-ethical destiny of the Jewish people. The 'holy city' becomes relative not by being rejected but by being taken up beyond itself.

It is this generally less acknowledged aspect that we are going to insist on — the essential Jerusalem where the three traditions once again find a common point of reference. And we ask to be allowed to follow more particularly the way of the eastern Christian tradition, which is more aware of this aspect of things. In so doing, we want to recover a common language which has rigorous intellectual and ontological meaning for the three communities of believers before it splits up and lapses into harmless sub-senses.

An example of this is the notion of *hospitality*. We have already brought out the fact that the ambiguity of Jerusalem is largely due to the politico-religious impulse to make an exclusive appropriation of a city which betokens an universality of another order. Closed or open city? Hospitable or inhospitable city? What emerges clearly from the whole Abrahamic tradition is that the reply depends upon the welcome offered to the Jerusalem of the future on the site of the one here 'on earth'. Abraham himself underwent that ordeal of hospitality which was to consecrate him as a believer and as an intercessor in the unfolding of revelation. It was on the occasion of the 'philoxenia' (love of the stranger) at Mambre (Gen. 18) that he received the divine visitation which Sodom and Gomorrah were to refuse.

In the perspective of the Christian faith, the 'explosion' of the earthly Jerusalem in the Spirit amounts to an extension of God's hospitality to the confines of being. It is true that for this faith there is a concrete sign of this welcome, and this is the Eucharist where the trace of the heavenly Jerusalem is made present in our space-time (by means of the *epiclesis*, the oriental tradition has it). 'The Lamb standing, as though it had been slain,' 'before the throne' (Rev. 5:6), image of the risen one and unique locus of the Eucharist celebration, signifies that God in the Eucharist Jesus compassionates (in the active sense of this word) *every man* who comes into the world (St Maximus the Confessor). This enables us to understand better why the fundamental ecclesiology has to be an ecclesiology of communion in the many senses of this word (Eucharist, local churches, collegiality). There is a sense in which the Church is wherever the Eucharist is enacted in the fullness of faith which is pre-supposes: its one and only centre remains that heavenly Jerusalem 'where no temple is to be seen, for its temple is the Lord God the Almighty and the Lamb' (Rev. 21:22). Any other 'centre' of authority or ecclesiastical jurisdiction (whether we call it Rome, Constantinople or Moscow) can only be provisional, under 'judgement' (in 'crisis'), subject to becoming more and more transparent on the Jerusalem-like model of communion in Christ 'until he comes again' . . . Now this return and the final refinding are also under the sign of hospitality. Is the discourse uttered by Christ at the final judgement (Matt. 25) anything else than a supreme recognition, on the threshold of the kingdom, of the infinite scope, simultaneously human and divine, of this hospitality: 'I was hungry, I was thirsty, I was naked, in prison, a stranger . . . and you welcomed me.' To translate this text as a pressing invitation to act 'charitably' alone certainly does not do justice to its true meaning. Hospitality here means an openness that is quite unconditional and unhedged about, even by an earthly Jerusalem, through an attentive desire to welcome the unpredictable God. It is to recognise that we are all equidistant from God and that another's mere being there is the inalienable place of God's own self-disclosure.

And this brings us back to the other attribute, enigmatic as it is, of Jerusalem, however differently this is seen in the three traditions: Jerusalem as 'mother' (Ps. 87:5: 'This one and that one were born in her'). This is what every town is — 'metropolis' in a certain way and by its own impetus: expansiveness, taking into one's care, protection. A religious centre has, therefore, all the more reason to be so perhaps: a metaphor of spendour, of apparent triumph and of assurance of security through belief. At the same time we need to remember how the prophets of the Old Testament insist on the work of compassion, of consolation of which Jerusalem is/is to be at one the object and the sign (Isa. 40 and, above all, 54).

2. THE INTERMEDIATE SIGN

The times inaugurated by the first century of our era hurls Jerusalem into the major crises of world history. It is no longer just a name written on a sacred text, a city on the horizon of our faith. The rise of the two universal religions of Christianity and Islam first of all, then the classical conflict of the nations, will cast it onto the unfurling waves of their successive clashes. In this way, the 'holy city' becomes a simple reference-point on the universal calendar. From this time on Jerusalem is no longer just within the horizon of three religions, but also somewhere *between* their respective territories of faith and life: an intermediate sign. It is an intermediate sign in another sense too, because, almost under our very eyes, Jerusalem picks out a way between a recognised past and an unknown future to which it is invited: once again it has to do what it has never found it easy to do — to declare itself for what it is.

Our survey of the centuries will have to be very brief . . . Let us just recall the Jewish vision of a Jerusalem in counterpoint with the state of diaspora which derives in main from the second century.

The 'memory' of the earthly Jerusalem does not disappear from the Jewish religion. How could it be otherwise? It is integrated into the central system of legal ordinances, the *mitzvot*, which are said to be incapable of complete observance except on the soil of the 'Holy Land' and of Jerusalem in the first place. And enumeration of them would take too long, and in any case be useless. *The traditionally important notions of 'exile' and 'return' undergo subtle changes of meaning as a result. Islam, for example, approaches them from quite a different angle of the faith. 'You are told: Return. But the idea of return implies that of some former presence, and woe to you if by place of return you understand Damascus, Baghdad or some other earthly homeland'* (Sahrawardi *Epistle of the Towers of the Citadel*). *Or take the famous saying of the imam Ja'afar (a saying that later became a hadith): 'Islam began in exile (in Medina) and it will go back into exile (in Jerusalem, last qibla) as it began; and blessed are those members of the community of Mahomet who will leave their homeland (in order to refind justice).'*

This is precisely how it is: historically speaking, the Muslim community touches the walls of the 'holy city'. Under Omar (632) Jerusalem entered into the *oikumene*, the universe, of Islam (dar-al-Islam). And from many points of view it was an exemplary entry. Preceded by four months of siege, it was accompanied by no destruction or violence: Sura 17, about the nocturnal ascension of the prophet, watches over the acts of the new conqueror. And the person who welcomes him is no ordinary person either. Sophronius, patriarch of Jerusalem, in the line of the bishops of the early Church of the Christian faith, a monk and a contemplative, was also an active mediator of reconciliation and peace between the ecclesiastical centres of his century.[7] He does not seem to have experienced the conquest as a crumbling of Christianity or as a demonstration of the superiority of Islam but simply as a turning-point in time, and as a face-to-face meeting of the two religions under the sign of the 'Jerusalem on high'. Further, Omar went as a pilgrim, not as the head of an empire: 'The caliph entered sitting on his camel and wearing a much used mantle' (Theophan *Chronographie* ed. Be Beer, p. 339). At the hour of prayer, Sophronius invited him to pray in the church of the *Anastasis,* but Omar refused, with the remark: 'If I prayed in your temple, you would lose it, for the Muslims would snatch it from you after my death saying: Omar prayed here' (Eutychius *Annals* P.G. 111, 1099c). The very first gesture of the caliph was to commit himself personally to clean the ancient enclosure of the Temple (*Haram al-Charif*) which had long been overlaid with a mass of refuse. Islam inaugurated its presence in Jerusalem with a modest oratory which Omar had built near the Rock of Abraham. In 691 the Omayyad caliph Abd al Malik built the Dome of the Rock (incorrectly called the Mosque of Omar) and, a short while afterwards, he himself (or his son)

K

built the great mosque at the southernmost point of the sacred enclosure, *al Aksa:* the imprint of Sura 17 is now made explicit and confirmed.

Muslim Jerusalem will never be a politico-religious centre but the concrete sign of its prophetic and eschatological orientation. The claims made about the town and its territory from time to time as a result of the vicissitudes of history by an Islam which felt itself 'excluded' express this sense very precisely, strongly rooted as it is in the living evidence of belonging to the community of Abraham.

For two major inscriptions that are veritable professions of Islamic faith are inscribed in Jerusalem. They are still there in the mosques of the *Haram al-Charif* and they make disturbing reading. The first is about Jesus and is to be found in the drum of the Dome of the Rock; it reads from east to west: 'O Mary, God announces to you the joy of a word from him: the Messiah, Jesus, Son of Mary, is his name' (Sura 3, 40). The second is to be found in the axial niche of the Aqsa and bears upon the conduct of God towards Mary: 'Every time Zachary found Mary in the sanctuary, he saw that she had food with her. And when he asked her: "Where does this food come from, Mary?", she replied: "From God who fills without measure all those whom he wills" ' (Sura 3, 37). And as for the question why God himself sustained Mary during her fast, Islam does not hesitate to say that it is so that she might enter into her 'quite unique' vocation (Sura 16, 77) as the virgin mother of the Messiah, Sïdna Aïssa, Our Lord Jesus.[8]

These 'intermediate signs' have apparently not always been received and deciphered with the understanding of the faith required by the places from which they spoke. It was not too long before Western Christianity which was still establishing itself — and not without some difficulty — exploded towards Jerusalem. The crusades: these constituted one of history's most successful tricks, because once the fervour and dash of the beginnings had dissipated on the way, what emerged was a humanity quite different from that which had believed it would triumph at the start. Earthly Jerusalem was the temporal pole of these great movements of lawlessness which went on for nearly four centuries. The term 'crusade' became as it were the brand image of a certain Western style of representing the cause of the Christian faith in the world. These are vicissitudes of history, in the largest sense of the word to be sure, but their consequences, such as we shall indicate briefly here, still weigh heavily on our consciences and on events. What happened was that for the first time the 'holy places' (the meaning of which Eastern Christianity, like Islam, had anchored above in the 'heavenly Jerusalem') became the object of an armed conflict waged with a view to demonstrating the superiority of one faith over another. The crusades re-enacted the first exterminations formerly perpetrated 'by divine right' on the land of Palestine, and this in a very precise and regressive way. Even more subtly, 'history', under-stood as a cumulative and continuing enterprise (for the crusades are simultaneously an idea that is potent and one that has shaped the Christian west) and the truth of the faith coalesce in such a way as to become homologous: when faith subsides, historical action continues to act in its name out of sheer inertia.

We do not, of course, want in any oversimplified way to make the crusade solely responsible for this massive installation of history in the domain of faith. It is more a matter of a symptom of concomitance in the course of the particular way in which western society developed during a phase of its own expansion which then also became the matrix and unique norm for the whole world. But if we recall our particular concern here, we cannot fail to notice the effacement of the other 'centres' in favour of the new centre of Rome (see, for example Innocent III's letter to the crusad-ers of the fourth crusade): Jerusalem becomes a fief of a 'Latin kingdom' (1099), just as Constantinople does a little later (1204). Beyond the disputable but, in the final analysis, transitory aspect of this first example of politico-religious colonialisation, the real break takes place at a deeper level. The ecclesiology of communion, which, as we have seen, was in some sense founded *on* Jerusalem, will gradually give way to an ecclesiol-ogy of jurisdiction and centralism. Local churches, from Jerusalem and Antioch and Constantinople and further north, will see their apostolic hierarchy replaced and duplicated by another, under the authority of Rome. This time the transformations reverberate further than one might think. A whole way of thinking, a whole concrete sense of the Church, will be displaced and redefined as an immediate or a delayed result of the ambiguous attraction exercised by the earthly Jerusalem on the Christian west at the turn of the millennium. For the latter, the universality of the faith will from now on seem to have to be mediated by an essentially historical institutional centre (the 'eternal city'), the specific role of which inevitably implies expansion and unification. As for Jerusalem, it is in some sense relegated to the periphery, especially from the sixteenth century. In order to return to the conscience and present awareness of the three religions, it will in the future have to get back in touch both with the tensions of its own history and with the ambiguities of its religious position.

3. WAITING . . .

The three religions seem to have been excessively slow to live out and understand just what it is at the very heart of their own faith that could have enabled them to recognise the place of the living God in the other in a way that could liberate them creatively from routine ways of thinking.

Everything virtually destined Jerusalem to be the place of meeting and peace above all others for the three communities (especially in our own time, characterised as it is by the many efforts at international rapprochment), and yet it is the prey of bitter and fallacious political claims which, at the very best, used the religious reference merely as a pretext. 'The separation between the state of Israel and its religion is unthinkable and undesirable . . ., in any case for some generations to come; our leaders will continue to need the moral justification of the Bible in order to base the rebirth of the Israelite people on divine law' (Prof. Walter Grab, of the university of Tel-Aviv: see *Le Monde Diplomatique* [January 1971] p. 8).

This is very perspicacious, but by that very token it invites us to go on, beyond appearances that are never questioned enough. The determining factor in this situation could rest fundamentally on the unequal *historic condition* of the actual state of the three communities (using the term historic condition in the precise sense of the level of political, economic and technological development, on the western model). Where they do not betray ignorance and remoteness, official ecclesiastical declarations about the 'Holy Land' are content to fall into step with previously formulated diplomatic positions. Eastern Christianity, which by its very being is probably most deeply rooted in the spiritual and concrete space surmounted by Jerusalem, has long kept a silent presence, and for the same 'historical' reasons. And it is only now that Islam, as we have said, is in the process of making a difficult come-back into the open history from which it was excluded. For the present, we have to recognise that the immediate future of Jerusalem seems to be in suspense until a nationalist movement, Zionism, western in make-up and biblical in tone, plays itself out. Is this history's last trick? For its desire to get back in touch with and to establish itself on the land of the near-east puts Israel back in an 'original' situation. It finds itself as it were at 'another beginning' of its religious awareness, summoned to understand and signify once more its fidelity not only to 'its God' but above all to its 'kind' (who in any case turn to the same God). Abrahamic hospitality emerges once again with all the forgotten gravity of the eschatological demands of faith, intelligence and life which it makes. It is true that the contrary impulse is still stronger in the pragmatic — and illusory — order of our world. This expresses itself in the alienation of others in the name of a power policy which intends to push them out of history once again. But does this alienation of others not expose Israel to the risk of alienating herself more and more from itself just in this corner of the world where she wants to refind herself?

In the final analysis, the essential options about Jerusalem remain the same: they have just become more pressing, more burning: 'O Jerusalem, Jerusalem . . . how often would I have gathered your children together

... and you would not' (Luke 13:34). 'And I saw the holy city, new Jerusalem, coming out of heaven from God' (Rev. 21:2).

Translated by John Maxwell

Notes

1. The name Jerusalem is dual: *Yerushalaïm*. Commentators have often seen in this fact a hint of its constitutive bipolarity.

2. It seems idle to speculate, as some people do, about the 'Abrahamic seam' of Islam that goes back to the genealogy of Agar (Gen. 16). This is a reference that is scarcely even metaphorical from our present point of view. What are much more interesting, on the other hand, are Schellings rather unexpected remarks about the 'archaic character' of Islam, the figure of Melchisedech and of the Johannine Jerusalem. See Schelling *Sammtliche Werke* ed. Cotta 11 p. 167.

3. These two expressions — 'to orientate oneself', 'to turn towards' — have a quasi-technical significance for the three spiritual traditions, as we shall be seeing.

4. Article 'Jerusalem' in Encyclopaedia Judaica (Jerusalem 1971) 9 coll. 1378 ff.

5. Islam is habitually credited with the institution of the 'holy war', but its position is in fact very clear. For Islam a military enterprise imposed by circumstances has only a subordinate, minor and provisonal value. Mahomet's *hadiths* (sayings) on his return from an armed expedition are well known: 'We have come back from the little holy war to the great holy war' (the spiritual combat). And in the same vein was his reply to somebody who asked him whether he could ensure his salvation by military heroism alone: 'No, not even if you fight to the very guard-hilt of your sword.'

6. As in the account of the transfiguration: 'And they spoke of his departure (*exodus*) which he was to accomplish at Jerusalem' (Luke 9:31).

7. See Christoph von Schöborn *Sophrone de Jérusalem* (Paris 1975).

8. Some authors maintain that Islam meant these inscriptions to make reparation for the Jewish polemics that presented Mary as an adultress. Berchochebas (132-135) during his revolt killed all Judaeo-Christians who refused to affirm this. See L. Massignon *Parole donnée* (Paris 1962) p. 269.

Contributors

JOSEPH COMBLIN was born in Brussels in 1923. He studied theology at Louvain, and was ordained priest in 1947. He has had experience as a parish priest in Belgium, Brazil and Chile. Since 1962, he has been a lecturer in theology in various faculties in Latin America; since 1971, he has also lectured in the theological faculty of the University of Louvain. His recent publications include: *The Meaning of Mission* (English version published 1977); *O Espirito na historia* (1979); *The Church and the National Security State* (English version published 1979). He is a regular contributor to the *Revista eclesiástica brasileira*.

RICHARD G. COTE, O.M.I., was born in 1934 at Lewiston (U.S.A.). He studied at the universities of Angers and Strasbourg, gaining a doctorate in theology in 1967. He has worked in Southern Africa for fifteen years, mainly in the teaching field of higher education and theology. Presently he is Associate Professor at Loyola University in New Orleans. His published works include *Could It Be?* and *Universal Grace: Myth or Reality?*

WILHELM DUPRÉ was born in 1936 in Hermeskeil, Germany. He has had the chair of the philosophy of religion in the university of Nijmegen since 1970, after having taught philosophy in the university of Vienna and also taught for nine years at DePaul University, Chicago. He has published many articles on the thinking of his fellow countryman, Nicholas of Cusa, and the philosophy of religion and anthropology, and his books include *Die Babinga Pygmäen* (1962), *Philosophisch-theologische Schriften des Nicolaus von Kues* (1964-1967) and *Religion in Primitive Cultures: A Study in Ethnophilosophy* (1975).

CHRISTIAN DUQUOC, O.P., was born in Nantes in 1926, and ordained in 1953. After various studies including those at the Ecole

126

Biblique in Jerusalem, where he gained his degree, followed by a doctorate in theology, he now teaches dogmatic theology at the Theology
Faculty in Lyon. He is a member of the editorial committee of the review
Lumière et Vie. His published books include *L'Eglise et le Progrès* and the
two-volume *Christologie* published in 1972.

JOST ECKERT was born in Düsseldorf in 1940. Since 1977 he has been
professor of New Testament in the Theological Faculty at Trier. He is
co-editor of the *Regensburger Neues Testament* and of *Biblische Unter-
suchungen*. His publications include: *Die urchristliche Verkündigung im
Streit zwischen Paulus und seinen Gegnern nach dem Galaterbrief* (1971).

WALTER KERN, S.J., studied at Freiburg, Pullach (near Munich),
Rome (philosophy) and Innsbruck (theology). From 1957 until 1969, he
taught the history of modern philosphy and the philosophical doctrine of
God at Pullach and since 1969 he has been teaching fundamental theol-
ogy at Innsbruck University. He has published *Atheismus – Marxismus –
Christentum* (1976, 2nd edn., 1979); *Disput um Jesus und um Kirche*
(1980); also articles on Hegel in *Scholastik/Theologie und Philosophie*,
Hegel-Studien and *Zeitschrift für Katholische Theologie*.

CHRISTOPHER F. MOONEY, S.J., was born in 1925 in the U.S.A.,
and ordained in 1957. He holds a doctorate in theology from the Institut
Catholique, Paris, and a doctorate in law from the University of Pennsylvania, Philadelphia. He is presently Assistant Dean at the University of
Pennsylvania Law School and his primary interest is the relationship
between religion and law. His published works are *Teilhard de Chardin
and the Mystery of Christ* (1966); *The Making of Man* (1971); *Man
Without Tears* (1975); *Religion and the American Dream* (1977).

IGNACE PUTHIADAM, S.J., is professor of Indian thought and comparative theology, in the Jesuit Faculties of Shembaganur, Pune and
Delhi. He has written *Come, Let Us Celebrate; Endlos ist die Zeit in
Deinen Händen* (with Dr. M. Kämpchen) and many articles in Indian and
foreign journals. He is also general editor of the Dialogue series.

ANSELME TITIANMA SANON is bishop of the diocese of Bobo-
Dioulasso in the Upper Volta. Born in Bobo-Dioulasso in 1937, he was
ordained a priest in 1962 and studied theology at the Gregorian University in Rome and sociology in Paris. His doctoral thesis was entitled
*Tierce Eglise, ma Mère, ou la conversion d'une communauté paienne au
Christ* (pub. 1970), and he writes widely in reviews, including *Cahiers
d'études africaines, Afrique et parole, Revue du clergé africain*.

$5.95

CONCILIUM
Religion in the Eighties

A multi-volume library of contemporary religious thought • published
in 10 volumes annually • exploring the
latest trends and developments in the Sociology of
Religion, Liturgy, Dogma, Practical Theology,
Fundamental Theology, Canon Law, Ecumenism,
Spirituality and Moral Theology

"A courageous and timely work. *Concilium* illumines the great issues of
today."

—*America*

"The most ambitious crash program ever undertaken in theological
re-education. The essays are uncompromisingly competent, solid, and
nourishing. *Concilium* is indispensable."

—*The Christian Century*

"A bold and confident venture in contemporary theology. All the best
new theologians are contributing to this collective summa."

—*Commonweal*

THE SEABURY PRESS, NEW YORK   T. &. T. CLARK, EDINBURGH